Living Singlish

How to Build a Fabulous Life As a Single Woman

Marne Platt

Living Singlish: How to Build a Fabulous Life as a Single Woman

©2020 by Marne Platt All Rights Reserved

ISBN-13: 9798730621145

Originally published in 2016 as Living Singlish: Your Life, Your Way. This book has been updated and revised.

Cover design by 100Covers

Dedicated to every woman, everywhere, of any age. You deserve the life of your dreams.

With thanks to the women who showed me the way.

Table of Contents

Introduction

Are you a young woman starting to build your adult life? Are you getting ready for your first real home away from family, and the first full-time job to pay for it all? There are so many decisions to make, and the right choices aren't always clear. You have tons of questions, but you're embarrassed to ask them. There might not even be one right answer.

Maybe it seems like all of your friends are more in control of their lives than you are. Some of them are getting married, many have long-term relationships; and maybe that's not for you right now. You want an exciting, independent life – a fabulous life as a single woman – but you're a little afraid that it won't happen. Maybe you want to fast-forward by 20 years or so, just to see how it all turns out.

Unfortunately, that peek into the future isn't possible, though wanting it is totally normal.

Living Singlish is the next best thing. In this book, you'll learn 7 simple principles that will help you prioritize, make decisions, and shape your life. They will also help you balance your needs and wants, fun and responsibility. The principles will help you decide what is important and what you can ignore, so you can focus on building the life you want.

How do I know all of this? Well, not so long ago, I was you. I'd been to college and graduate school and was starting the career I had always dreamed of. I found a job, a place to live, and started my life as a grown-up. My life looked fabulous from the outside and, in many ways, it was. But I was secretly scared, and I wished desperately to look into the future and know what the consequences of some of my decisions would be. I built a great life, with close friends, exciting vacations, interesting work and tons of fun; it's been worth the moments of inner panic. But I made some mistakes along the way that you don't have to make.

This book grows out of a discussion I had with a younger colleague, who is a lot like you. Let's call her Jillian (it's not her real name). Jillian was looking for her first apartment that she would live in by herself. She had always lived at home, in dorms, or with friends or boyfriends. Now, at 26, it was time to go out on her own. She knew exactly what she wanted in the apartment: location, size, which way the windows should face...but she didn't know anything about her budget, how much things like heat, electricity and internet access would cost, or what it would take to furnish her new home. We ended up talking a lot about how you run your life on your own, when there is no one else to look after the bills, plan for the future, or be your "safe date" for parties and trips.

After several weeks of repeating the same things, I realized that there were just a few basic guidelines that made it easier. The more I talked with friends, the more I realized that we were all following the same rules without talking about it. Those unwritten rules became the Singlish Principles, and what started as a letter of advice to Jillian became this book.

The Singlish principles will show you how the successful, confident single women you see around you became that way. You'll learn how we prioritize, how we plan, how we present ourselves to the world so that everyone else can see how special we are. You'll learn how we balance work and fun, and how we balance what's important to do now versus what can wait.

When you follow the Singlish principles, you'll become stronger, more confident, and more capable. You will learn from the experiences of other women, some of them famous and some of them just like you and me. And you will begin to build the life you want for yourself, not the life that other people think you should live. Best of all, the book is for you as an individual; the principles can apply to every woman, but I wrote the book with single women in mind.

I promise that if you read this book, you will learn how to use these principles to improve your life. If you follow them, you will find yourself calmly making the decisions that used to intimidate you, taking on and mastering new challenges, and having loads of fun. Before you know it, you will be the kind of woman that other women look up to, because you will be living your life, your way!

Sitting and thinking about how scary the future is won't make you stronger. Don't let life get ahead of you. Make your own decisions, create the life you want. Start living the Singlish way.

The Singlish Attitude

"You have to face things, have faith in what you do and go for it."

Annie Lennox, Musician

"Be your own person, be independent."

Ruth Bader Ginsburg, US Supreme Court Justice

Two women are having lunch in a cafe. Although different in age, they look very much alike. The older woman, perhaps in her 40s, wears jeans, high-heeled boots, and a cashmere sweater. Her reddish-brown hair is cut fashionably short. She speaks confidently, smiles broadly, and laughs a lot.

The younger woman also wears jeans, with low boots and a cotton sweater. Her long brown hair is held back in a single braid. She is full of questions, smiles and laughs but without quite as much flair as her older friend. Still, they seem so much alike, so in tune with one another that you would think they were sisters. Let's hear what they are saying….

Younger Woman: Tell me again who you are?
Older Woman: I am you, Lizzie, just 20 years older. Everyone but my closest friends calls me Elizabeth now. I'm always with you, because I have always been inside you. I remember what it was like to be you. So you can ask me anything. I'll never make fun of you, or think you are silly, because I had the same fears. I know you can do what it takes to be whoever you want to be, because I did it.
Lizzie: You seem so confident! What were you ever afraid of?
Elizabeth: Well, when I finished school I was afraid that I wouldn't find a job, let alone one that I liked and that would pay enough to do more than just cover the bills. I worried about finding new friends, and about making a life for myself. I didn't really want to get married and I wasn't sure about children, and I was afraid that I couldn't make it on my own.
Lizzie: That sounds like me! I don't want a boyfriend right now, and I can't even imagine getting married, let alone having children . I wonder if I will be good at my job, I worry about where I will live and how to save money. I worry about how to make friends if I move to a new city. Did you really worry about all of that too?

Elizabeth: Of course I did. That's why I came back to talk to you. I wanted you to know that it's not that hard. There are a few principles you can follow. If you do, you will make the best decision you can at the time. If something goes wrong, you will know how to recover. You will grow into someone like me — actually you will grow into me — without as much worry and stress as I had.

Lizzie: Are you the only one like this? I mean, are any of your friends also single and happy? All of my friends seem to want to get married. I feel like I am the only one who thinks it's not for me. I can't really talk with my friends about it; I don't know if they will understand.

Elizabeth: There are lots of women like me. They all grew from women like you. At your age it can still be hard to talk about not fitting the traditional picture of wanting the big white wedding. Don't worry about it, and don't ever wish for something you don't really want, just because someone else thinks you should want it. I can tell you about lots of my friends, and even some famous women, who decided to live a Singlish life. There are more of us than you realize.

Lizzie: It's hard to believe that I could ever be like you…

Wouldn't it be great to have your older, more confident self nearby any time you had a question? You could ask her anything, and she would give you a straight answer, without making you feel embarrassed. She could help you learn how to make decisions, overcome your fears about adult life, and enjoy yourself.

You can find her in this book. If you are a woman starting your adult life, this book can be your older self. Ask anything; the 7 Singlish principles will help you find the answer.

Right now, you're probably either finishing university or starting your first "serious" job. Maybe you are ready to set up your first home, with or without roommates. Whether you are partnered or single, wealthy or struggling financially, doesn't matter. All that matters is that you are about to take the big leap into adult life, you have a lot of questions, and you aren't sure where to turn for practical answers to help you build the life you want. Follow the principles in the book. You will develop a Singlish attitude and before you know it, you will be living a Singlish life.

Why Singlish?

Singlish comes from 2 perspectives: Single and Not Single

Singl- because these are the skills, facts and attitude a single woman needs to look after herself, and not be dependent on anyone else to put a roof over her head, food on the table, and a stimulating challenge in front of her brain. These are the basics for a fulfilling life as a single woman.

-ish because the same skills, facts and attitude give you the same advantages if you have a partner, as well as the confidence to know that you can

make it on your own. They are just as important for partnered women as they are for single women.

What is a Singlish Attitude?

Having a Singlish attitude means taking control of your own life and taking responsibility for how much enjoyment you get out of it. Singlish women choose the life they want, and then take steps to build it. The Singlish woman of any age makes her own decisions, plans her own life, and makes the most of her opportunities. She enjoys the good times, copes with bad times, and lives a full and interesting life as she defines it.

Singlish women don't live their lives on autopilot, letting someone else take the decisions that affect their futures. Remember, you are responsible for how your life turns out. Yes it can be scary. It's also a powerful feeling, knowing that you can make such important decisions for yourself. Who knows your wishes better?

There are millions of Singlish and potential Singlish women in the world. According to research by the Pew Research Center in 2019,[35] 31% of American women of all ages are single. Looking at it by age, 32% of women 18-29 years old, 19% of women aged 30-49 and 49% of women over 65 are single.

If you're not single right now, chances are you will be at some point in your life, whether by chance or by choice. What do you want that life to look like? Do you want to be strong, independent, and in control? Do you want to create the life you want, with new experiences, fun, and success? You are not alone.

As far back as 150 years ago, strong women were pointing out to the rest of us that we created many of our own limitations. The law in those years prevented married women (and we were all supposed to get married) from owning property, entering contracts, and controlling our own money, even if we had earned it ourselves or inherited it from our families.

For centuries, the ideal middle class or elite woman was considered little more than a vessel for producing children. She had no right to own property or sign contracts. An unmarried woman had to live at home, or with some other "protective" family member(s), living her life in service to their needs as a governess, or as a devoted caregiver to elderly relatives. Unmarried working-class women were usually domestic servants, cleaning and cooking for someone else, and often living in a tiny room in the attic. Men thought women were fragile, easily overexcited, or incapable of making rational judgments.

Women who fought these stereotypes were considered crazy. The word hysterical, which is still a label given to women who fight passionately for something they believe is right, originated from the idea that the woman's uterus was diseased, making her mind sick too.

Fortunately, times changed. Single women can now take advantage of all life has to offer. The Singlish woman does it with gusto. She looks after herself, makes her own choices, and lives the life she wants. She doesn't have to "serve" anyone in order to justify her existence and doesn't have to depend on anyone else to make important decisions or provide her with money so she can survive.

Elizabeth Cady Stanton, the famous activist for women's equality in the 1800s, once wrote about assumptions of female inequality, "The worst feature of these assumptions is that women themselves believe them." [40] To Elizabeth, it was about attitude. When we accept that others know more about what's right for us than we do, we make ourselves childlike.

Letting go of those assumptions makes you stronger, more Singlish. When we let go of the myth that "women aren't good at that" we take responsibility for ourselves and our own lives. It's a fundamental part of the Singlish attitude.

Being a Singlish woman can sound a lot like being a stereotypical man. Like women, most men make choices about their lives that consider the needs of their loved ones. But if a man chooses a job, relationship, or activity based mostly on what's right for him alone, expecting his family to adjust, no one is surprised. This even holds true among highly educated couples. A 2014 survey of Harvard MBA graduates[18] found that the man's career usually became the lead career. That was true even if the couple had agreed that it wouldn't be that way.

If that's not what you want for your life, you need to follow the Singlish principles, whether you remain single or find a partner. Being Singlish means having the confidence to fulfill your own needs and wishes, and to recognize that as your right.

How is Singlish Different Than Single?

Being Singlish is not the same as being single.

To quote Judy Ford, in her book Single: The Art of Being Satisfied, Fulfilled and Independent, "being single is not a condition to be cured."[20] I love that line; it really sums up for me that being single is a fact, not a judgment. It does not give anyone else the right to judge you.

Being single means not being partnered, with a spouse, a common-law spouse, a civil partner, or a long term (or short term) informal companion. Single women may live alone, or with someone else: friends, relatives, or children.

Being single doesn't have to be permanent, either. There is no age at which a single woman becomes too old to find a loving partner if she wants one and is physically and mentally able to engage in a relationship.

Being Singlish is different. Living Singlish means recognizing that, whether you are alone or in a relationship, you are a whole person with valid needs, wishes, skills and abilities, fully capable of making decisions and steering your own life.

Being Singlish doesn't mean giving up on love, or on dating, or on children, or on life. Nor does it mean that you must focus on your career to the exclusion of everything else. You can be Singlish and single, Singlish and paired or married, or single and not Singlish. Still, most Singlish women are single, if not for their entire adult lives than for significant stretches of time.

Being Singlish can mean getting off the dating treadmill when you don't want to date and hopping back on if someone interesting comes along. It might mean getting married someday. Or it might mean getting divorced. Either way, it's your life and these are your choices.

For you, living Singlish may mean having a child by yourself by any of the many means available to women these days. Or it may mean for you, as it did for me, acknowledging that children are just not what you are looking for out of life. And again (assuming your biology will cooperate) you can change your mind at any time. Being Singlish is ultimately about choice, freedom, and self-determination.

I believe there is a Singlish woman in each woman on the planet. You need only look inside to find her.

There have always been Singlish women in the world. These women broke society's restrictive bonds and carved meaningful lives for themselves. Some were famous women whose names and lives are well-known. Others were known only to their friends and family.

In this book we'll meet a few of them: strong, independent women, living by the basic Singlish principles: know who you are and what you want, make your own decisions, and run your own life. Their experiences can inspire us, instruct us, and give us hope when things are tough. There are Singlish women around you every day. There's a Singlish woman inside you. All you need to do is let her out.

First let's rejoin our two women in the cafe.

Lizzie: OK, I guess I believe that you are really me. I still have a hard time believing that I can turn out as confident as you are, but I suppose I can give it a try. I have so much to ask you! First of all, you mentioned easy principles that I can follow. What are they?

Elizabeth: I'm so glad you believe me! You'll see, it's really pretty simple. There are 7 basic principles for living a Singlish life. I'll tell you what they are, and each time we work on one of your questions, we'll refer to the most important ones for that situation. The seven principles are…:

The Seven Singlish Principles

1. **Know who you are** The Singlish woman doesn't try to be anyone else. She knows her own strengths and flaws and is comfortable in her own skin.

2. **Know what you want** Singlish women know their own minds. They know what they do want, and also what they don't want, from life, work, and relationships. Singlish women take advice but don't necessarily do what the last person they spoke with thinks is right. The Singlish woman goes after what she wants, and won't be pushed into doing something that isn't right for her.

3. **Stand by your decisions** Once a Singlish woman makes a decision, she sticks with it unless there is a really good reason to change. If she's chosen a hard path, she doesn't give up easily. She knows that overcoming adversity brings strength.

4. **Have fun, celebrate success** Singlish women know that fun is an important part of life. They remember that every success, big or small, is worth recognizing as a step along the right path.

5. **Look after yourself** That means planning for now and for later, and not waiting for Prince Charming, or anyone else, to appear and take care of your "forever after." A Singlish woman takes care of who she is today, and of the woman she will be tomorrow.

6. **Always tell yourself the truth** Being honest with yourself, even if the truth is hard to face, is an important part of taking responsibility for your own life. When a Singlish woman makes a mistake, she admits it, learns from it, and tries not to make the same mistake again. She doesn't constantly remind herself of past errors; she knows there is no point in that.

7. **Just try** The Singlish woman knows that she can do more than other people might think. Even if something is a bit scary, if it feels right, she gives it a try. No waiting for, or needing, anyone else's permission!

Sounds serious, maybe even a little scary, doesn't it? Don't be afraid. You can do this in small steps, and with each step, you will become more confident. In the next chapter I'll describe a Singlish woman for you. This one happens to be me. In the meantime, let's see what the two women in the cafe are talking about…

Lizzie: So if I understand, you, Elizabeth, are really me, Lizzie. And you are telling me that if I just stick with a few principles, develop this Singlish attitude, I can deal with all of these worries I have and have the life that I want?
Elizabeth: Yes, that's right. I'm not promising you that it will all be easy. But you can do it. There's a Singlish woman in you, and I am the proof.

My Singlish Life: One Woman's Story

"...the greatest single strength a human being can possess: knowing what you can live with and what you can't live with - and why. That, I came to realize, is independence."

Vivian Gornick, "What Independence Has Come to Mean For Me" in The Bitch in The House (Cathi Hanauer, ed)

"I am a strong woman with or without this other person, with or without this job, with or without these tight pants"

Queen Latifah, rapper, singer, actress, talk show host and TV producer

This book is about you, not about me. But I did think it would be good to give you a bit of background, and an example of how you can become Singlish and what it can mean to your life.

I grew up in an upper middle-class home near New York City. My parents are both college-educated business owners with interests ranging from history to sociology, gardening to technology. I have one sister, a lawyer. She is divorced and now in a long term relationship. As far as I know, she has no plans to get married again. She's a Singlish woman.

We were raised to take responsibility for ourselves. We had chores and we did them. Homework was not optional either, even if no one was home when we got there after school. I was a 1970's latchkey child. So were most of my friends. We turned out fine. If we needed help with our homework, we asked Mom or Dad when they got home. If they couldn't help us, we had teachers, friends, and of course the library, where we went weekly, as a family. The love of reading and the ability to teach myself have stayed with me; I think they are huge advantages that anyone can develop.

Financial awareness was part of our education, right from the beginning. We received an allowance, in payment for completing our chores. It financed trips to the movies with friends, souvenirs on vacations, almost anything we wanted, within reason. But there were no advances; we had to save our money, or do other tasks, like copying and filing in Dad's office, to earn more. I spent every summer from age 5-16 with my grandparents, and they reinforced the same rules, with one exception: my grandfather would give me the change if I went grocery shopping with him. Thanks to my grandfather, I often came home with more money than I had brought with me. Who in the world is better than a grandparent?

We had to put some of our earnings into a bank account. Back then you could have a joint bank account with your parents if you were under 18, so we each got one as soon as we could write our names legibly. I saved from my allowance and from jobs throughout school, even if it was just a few dollars at a time. I started trading stocks with pretend money, following my results in the newspaper, before I was 10. When I turned 16 I started doing it for real, using some of the money that I had saved over the years.

I always knew that I would have a career, and I learned about working from my parents. I went to work with both of them, learning to do everything from bank statement reconciliations to running activity sessions for the elderly to selling cosmetics. That helped me decide what I wanted to do when I grew up. At first, when I was 5, I wanted to be a jockey. When Mom and Dad pointed out the terrible lifestyle involved, I decided that I would rather be a horse doctor, and never changed my mind.

My parents supported my decision; indeed, I was very fortunate that they supported ME, through college and veterinary school, until I had my first full-time job. During those years I had one most important task: do well in school and learn the skills I would need to take care of myself and be successful in life. Working as a veterinary nurse during college and veterinary school didn't pay much but it was great hands-on training and I saved as much as I could. I was very fortunate to have a safety net that gave me a lot of confidence, the push to succeed, and the skills to take care of myself.

Gloria Steinem quotes a female taxi driver in her book, *Outrageous Acts and Everyday Rebellions* as saying "Most women are one man away from welfare." [41] I don't think my parents had heard the phrase, but I was raised from the beginning not to be one of those women who needed a man to do everything for me. They felt I had too much talent and intelligence to let it go to waste, and it was my responsibility to make something of myself in the wider world.

If you have similarly supportive parents, or someone else who fills that role, take a minute now to thank them.

While my parents would have been happy to see me married to a good man, maybe even with children, they always expected that I would have a career, interests, and a life focused on doing something meaningful outside my home too.

Anyway, this isn't supposed to be a detailed story of my life, so let's fast forward. College, veterinary school, veterinary practice, a move to the pharmaceutical industry and onto the corporate ladder I jumped.

Along the way I had plenty of boyfriends, some very serious, some not so serious. One even had custody of his two children, making me an Instant Stepmom at 28. This was really eye-opening! If you are a woman who can take on someone else's young children and try to raise them as you would your own, I salute you. I couldn't do it.

Somewhere around age 30 I realized that I don't like looking after small children for long periods, and around 35, I realized that a part-time relationship, or a single life, had a lot of benefits for me. So here I am. On my own, I have:

- Moved around the US, and to Canada, Switzerland, and Australia
- Bought and furnished a house, and learned to do repairs on it
- Earned an MBA while working
- Learned another language
- Made friends from all walks of life, from many parts of the world,
- Seen many of the world's great sights
- Broadened my political horizons
- Become a confident public speaker
- Become a more discerning wine drinker and better cook

- Become a stronger and more empathetic person

I have learned an incredible amount about myself and the world – and I am not done yet!

Right now I live alone, work hard but not to the point of exhaustion, play hard but not to the point of stupidity. I travel the world for vacation or stay home if that's what I want. I date if I feel like it, and don't date if I am not in the mood. I am very picky about with whom I will share my precious private time, so there are often long stretches between relationships. By long stretches I mean years, and that's OK. Better to be alone and enjoy the company than to be attached to a man I dread seeing.

My life is a lot of fun right now. I value the independence of being able to go where and when I want to, too much to give it up. I've started riding after a 20-year hiatus, taken ballroom dancing lessons, joined a choir, and started an exercise program (several times, like most of us. But as you pass 40 you really have to get serious about it).

If it sounds like fun, it is. If it sounds scary, well, yes, it has been at times. And if it sounds lonely, sure I have my blue days. But they pass, and overall I love my life. That's what it means to be Singlish!

The Singlish life can be rewarding, exciting and fulfilling – it certainly has been for me. I will not look back on my life and say "that was boring! I wish I had… (you fill something in here)."

Living Singlish does require taking responsibility for yourself and your decisions. To help you decide if it's right for you, we'll go through the important stuff in the next chapters.

Friendships

Let's see what Lizzie and Elizabeth are talking about now....

Lizzie: You keep mentioning all of your friends. I don't think I have nearly as many as you do. How did you meet them? What do you do together? How did you get to be so close?

Elizabeth: You are right, Friends are important for a full life, and I do spend a lot of time with mine. Friends are important for three of the Singlish principles, too: looking after yourself, trying new things, and celebrating successes.

We all need friends. Friends make life more fun, they give us social outlets and stimulation, and help connect to the world beyond our doors. Who hasn't felt better after sharing a problem with a friend, or felt happier and more relaxed after laughing with one? Real friends, the people you make an effort to stay in contact with through moves, new jobs, and life's changes, help make your own life full and happier.

If you lived through the COVID-19 lockdowns, when we couldn't see our friends easily, you know how important these connections can be. Take a moment now to think of a friend you haven't talked with in a while and get in touch with them. You'll both be happy that you did.

You already know that there are many kinds of friends. Look at your own circle: you have friends who are very close, some not so close, and some who you see at particular events but not in between. That's completely normal. The Singlish woman has a broad range of interests and skills; her friends will too.

The most important thing is finding the right friends. Friends who accept your Singlishness, encourage you try new things and celebrate your successes. You want friends you can talk with and laugh with, and friends you can rely on when you have a bad day or need help.

At first, many of your friends will be single. Over time, some will marry or find long-term partners. You might love their partners, or you might not. That doesn't matter. What matters is that you and your friend have enough in common that you both value your time together, and you make time for each other. Even when your friends have partners, you and your friend can do things together, even go away on vacation, without them.

Some of your other friends may be single, and some will be living Singlish lives. Some of your married friends will become single again, by chance or by choice. That's your opportunity to support them through the changes, and teach them what you've learned about living a fabulous Singlish life.

Friends can come from any background and don't have to know anything about what you do for a living. They just have to be fun, warm, interesting and tolerant of your quirks. I count among my closest friends several other Singlish women from various countries, one woman with a happy marriage and 4 kids and a career as a fitness trainer, one woman with an average marriage and a job that she doesn't want to use to get up the ladder, one highly trained woman who dropped out of the rat race to raise her kids and follow her husband, one career woman with trailing husband, one divorced woman in no rush to find a new husband, one gay man in business for himself who can't find the right partner but hasn't quit trying…people of all ages, races, genders and persuasions, whose company I enjoy and who don't expect me to fit any particular mold. These are people I can call with my happiness, my successes, my trials and tribulations, and even if they don't understand exactly what I am talking about, they are happy for me or sympathetic, if need be.

A Singlish woman's friend sounds just like the friends that "regular" women have, don't they? Good. That's exactly the point.

See your friends regularly. Try new activities, go places, eat new foods, see new movies, meet new people and make new friends. Talk, laugh, commiserate, debate: friends are important for any life, Singlish or not.

Friends are important for other, more practical reasons, too. Friends are one another's rescuers in emergencies: if the power goes out, a car breaks down, or your flight is cancelled, there is someone you can contact so you don't feel alone, and someone who knows where you are and can help you deal with the situation. If the water heater stops working and the repair service can't come for a week, a friend can help you stay clean and presentable.

A trusted friend should have a copy of the keys to your home (and the code to the alarm, if you have one), in case you are ever locked out. On my first morning in my first house, I locked myself out.

No one had my new key, so I had to break a window to get back in – an expensive start! You can be sure that I gave my closest friend my house key the next day.

Friends Are Good For Your Health

It's just plain common sense that friends make life better. It's also common sense that a happier life is better than a sad and lonely one. Science backs this up.

Many studies show that people live longer and better with social connections. Doing things with friends keeps you more connected to the world around you, increases your feeling of belonging, is good for your self-esteem, and can help you to cope with difficulties. Friends can even help you start, or continue, healthy habits like eating well and exercising. Plus seeing your friends is fun.

A study in the US found that adults of any age, from early 20s to 90s, who spent more time out of the house in social pursuits lived healthier lives.[8] So get out, see your friends, have more fun, and stay healthier.

Having friends becomes even more important when you get older. One study of older adults found that people who were involved in mental, social, or productive activity had less risk of dementia. The authors concluded that social interaction and intellectual stimulation could help preserve mental function in the elderly.[48]

Another study of men and women aged 65 or over in Spain found that people who had fewer social ties and less interaction with others had a higher risk of cognitive decline. Interestingly, engaging with friends, as opposed to relatives, seemed to protect women, but not men, against cognitive decline.[49] This reinforces how important it is for women to have and maintain interests outside the home, and have many friends; it may keep your brain working better, for longer.

New Adventures, New Friends

It's pretty clear, friends are valuable as well as fun. How do you find your friends? Well, most of us have friends with whom we grew up: friends from our first school years, or from your university or college. You can find new friends in your neighborhood, or at the gym, or in clubs, or anyplace you go to regularly. Join a course at the local community college, or a book club through the library. You'll already have something in common with the other members, making it easier for the introverts among us to start a conversation. If you run, try a new route or a new time. Think about what you like to do, then look for opportunities to do it with new people.

Marilyn and Karin: Learning to Ski

Marilyn and Karin, now 27, have been friends since university. Karin is an avid skier, and always told Marilyn about how much fun she had on ski trips and how beautiful the mountains are. She invited Marilyn at least twice a year, but Marilyn always said no. Finally, Marilyn agreed to try.

Karin was thrilled to introduce her closest friend to her favorite activity. They bought Marilyn the right clothes, rented the right equipment, and arranged for a morning of introductory lessons. That afternoon, they skied together. Marilyn's instructor taught her to steer and stop, and Karin chose only easy slopes. Marilyn loved the fresh air and scenery, and she liked talking to people on the lifts. By the end of the day, she was hooked!

Now Marilyn and Karin ski together at least 3 or 4 times a year. Marilyn has new friends that she made through a local ski club. She has visited new places and met new people, none of whom care that she is not an expert skier. Marilyn doesn't care either – she is having too much fun.

Talk with your neighbors and the people you see regularly in stores. Talk to the baristas at your favorite coffee shop, or the other people who are usually there when you are. One woman I know struck up a conversation with the woman next to her on a long checkout line. Their conversation moved from the reason for the delays, to what it was keeping them from doing, to what other things they would rather be doing…and before long they had agreed to meet for a coffee, which became a regular event. Friends are out there if you open yourself up to finding them.

If you work outside your home, you will meet more new people at your workplace. Keep in mind that friends at work are not the same as friends outside of work. It's common to have business acquaintances. You might become close with them if you work together over a long time or in intense situations. Many of your conversations will be about work topics, with outside matters like family or hobbies only coming up occasionally. You might lose touch with them if you, or they, change jobs, even within the same company. That's fine; these friendships help make work more enjoyable, and they can certainly be good for your career. If any of your work friends grow into personal friends, be grateful for it. It doesn't always happen. Enjoy your work friends for who they are and let them enrich your life.

One thing you should know: despite the increasing numbers of women in the workplace, depending on the type of work you do, many of your business friends could be men. That's fine - I have plenty of male and female business friends. Realize that you may have to deal with the occasional wrong expectations or jealous wives. We'll talk about this later.

Elsa: Celebrating Success

Elsa is a geologist at an oil company. In the last few years she has become interested in working in marketing. She was turned down several times for marketing jobs because she had no business background. So at 32, she enrolled in an executive MBA program and went back to school while working. Those two years were unbelievably busy. Elsa spent most of her time studying with her classmates, some of whom became good friends. Her closest friends cheered her on and tried to help where they could.

Finally, just after her 34th birthday, Elsa graduated with her MBA. Her friends made her a graduation party with a big cake. Elsa spent the night catching up with people who were proud of her. She felt even better about her degree. It was worth all of the hard work.

Six months later, Elsa applied for and was appointed to a job in the marketing department. Now she had another reason to celebrate with her friends!

Life is richer, more interesting and more exciting with friends. Whether you prefer a huge circle of friends, a few close confidantes, or something in between, make the effort to stay connected. Friends really are the glitter that makes life sparkle!

Lizzie: Wow, I knew it was good to have friends but I never knew it was actually healthy! I already do a lot of things with my friends: I go to the gym with Jeanine, study with Melinda and Sonja, and Deborah taught me to cook. It will be harder if we live farther away after university, but I guess I'll find new friends. We'll have fun, try new things and celebrate success.

Elizabeth: Excellent, those are important Singlish principles for building solid friendships.

Applying Singlish Principles to Friendship

- Having fun and celebrating your successes is even better with friends
- Look after yourself: Spending time with friends is good for your mental and physical health.
- Try new things with your friends. It will expand your life and you might find a new hobby or interest.

Romance and Relationships

Conversation is getting very animated between our two women…what are they talking about?

Lizzie: You say that you aren't dating anyone. I don't really want to date anyone seriously right now, but what happens later? If I don't meet someone in university, where will I ever meet him? How do I find a man and also live this Singlish life you keep talking about?

Elizabeth: It sounds scary right now, doesn't it? I know how you feel. When I turned 30, and I wasn't dating anyone, I thought that was it for me. I had a couple of really sad days where I thought, 'I'll never find a man, it's the end of my life!" Let me tell you, that's not true.

First of all, it is possible to meet men after you leave university, if you want to. I personally am not that worried about it. I'm certainly not going to settle for dating a guy I'm not happy with, just to have a boyfriend. You become more selective. You realize that being without a date is fine and can even be more fun. It's much better to be out with friends or home doing something I enjoy than out on a bad date, or with a man who doesn't treat me as well as I deserve.

Lizzie: I don't know about that, I can't imagine even going to the movies alone, let alone going out for a meal by myself. And what if all of my friends have boyfriends or husbands and I don't?

Elizabeth: Here's how I learned to get past those fears. It starts with just two of the Singlish principles: Knowing what want, and always telling yourself the truth...

Bella DePaulo says, "adult humans need not come in matched sets."[14] Even if you eventually marry, chances are good that you will spend a portion of your life single, either before you marry or afterwards, due to divorce or your husband's death.

A good romantic relationship can be a plus in your life, but it's not an absolute requirement for happiness.

Women and men in the US are, on average, marrying about 5 years later than they did in the past. In 2009, 15% of women had never married. Of all women in 2009, 62% were married, 38% were not [47]. So if you choose not to marry, you are not alone.

Being Singlish doesn't mean that you never date, or that you never have another boyfriend, or never have sex. That's why you are Singlish, not celibate, or that outdated and judgmental word, a spinster. If you choose not to date, it's certainly fine. Being Singlish means that while you may date, or have a long distance relationship, or anything in between or on either side of the spectrum, you are comfortable with your choice, and with your life alone between those moments of romance.

The Singlish woman may at various points in her life want a partner, or want to date. That doesn't mean giving up her Singlish credentials. She takes the principles of Singlish living with her into the dating world. The Singlish principles help her make better choices as she looks for love. She knows what she wants and what she doesn't, and tells herself the truth about whether the relationship can work.

The Singlish woman might like to get married one day. Or she might not.

A married Singlish woman takes care of her own needs, steers her own life, considering her family's needs and wishes but never letting them block out her own needs and wishes completely.

Know what you want don't want in a relationship. Be absolutely, brutally honest with yourself about it. Don't give in to what someone else thinks you should want.

One very important aspect of being Singlish is that you don't want a partner so badly that you will accept anyone, just to avoid being alone. If that's where you are right now, you're not Singlish yet. Take heart though; you can be, if you follow the advice in this book.

And then there's sex. Singlish women generally like sex, because they like and respect themselves. They are just picky about their partners. In a loving relationship, sex can be one of the most beautiful ways a couple can show their love to one another, and quite a lot of fun. In a more casual relationship, it can combine fun with caring, if not a deep life commitment.

Well into the twentieth century, single women were expected to live entirely without sex. Women who chose not to follow that rule risked social ostracism, particularly if they became pregnant. Now, thanks to the availability of effective birth control, and the relaxation of some of these archaic social restrictions, many women are able to enjoy sex "outside of marriage." As if marriage was a big building that any women who wants sex has to pay to enter. The Singlish woman knows what she wants, whether that is a deep emotional attachment or a bit of fun and she shapes her sex life accordingly.

Let's look at the traditional dating scene through a Singlish lens.

One of the greatest freedoms of Singlish life is the freedom to decide whether, when, and whom to date without worrying about anyone else's opinion about what you 'should' do.

There will be times when you really don't feel like being in a relationship. You may have too much going on with work or friends, or you might not feel like going through the effort of finding someone worthwhile. That's fine. When you don't feel like dating, don't date. And don't let anyone make a big deal about it. I tell people "my head's in a different place right now" if they ask, and if I feel like explaining. These periods can last days, weeks, months, years. However long they last, just enjoy living your life without feeling the pressure to be part of a couple.

When (or if) the time comes that you do want to date, look inside yourself first. Start by knowing what you are looking for. Do you want a committed relationship, a fling, or something in between? Know what's important to you and remember that you deserve to have it. You should be treated with respect, consideration, and good manners all the time. A Singlish woman is a rare catch; she knows her worth, can look after herself and is confident and interesting. If she chooses a man, he's the lucky one.

One of the advantages I have found about long periods of singlehood between relationships is that I've had the time to think about what I really want, including those areas in which I will or will not compromise. It helps me weed out the bad fits quickly. I think it is fairer to the man, too.

The key Singlish principle here is to know what you want, and what you don't. Find the partner who provides that. Don't accept just anyone, even if he is rich, tall, good-looking, or all three. Know what you are looking for. If that changes, be honest with yourself about it and adapt accordingly.

Once you are ready, it's time to find someone. My discussion here is about finding a man, because that's where I have experience, but according to my gay and lesbian friends it's not that different for same sex partners. I think human nature is similar across genders, orientations, religions and cultures.

Make sure you are looking in the right places and giving out the right signals. A meeting of religious people devoted to restoring family values is not the right place to find a one-night stand.

Finding a man can be harder once you leave school. Work is the obvious starting place, but workplace romances are risky. Many companies frown on them, with good reason. They can bring unnecessary drama to the office, and firms may take some strange steps to prevent them. I worked at one company where the official policy on two associates dating required that they ask their managers for permission. You can imagine how well the employees adhered to that one.

If you do choose to date a colleague, the publicity can be tough. People will gossip about you, and any change in your performance (positive or negative) will be credited to or blamed on the relationship. You may feel like you are living in a fishbowl, with everyone else watching. If you work together and the relationship ends, it can be hard to avoid ugly public scenes. Most of the workplace romances I know about ended up with one or both of the parties leaving the company.

If you date someone higher up the management chain, you may run into some prejudices: any promotion is "obviously" because you are sleeping with the boss, not because of your skills. Many companies also have explicit policies preventing relationships within managerial lines to prevent sexual harassment, and I support that. The power differential is always there.

In my experience, these relationships almost always end badly. If that happens, or your relationship becomes public, the woman is almost always the one who pays the price. She may be fired or forced out, and her reputation is the one that takes the hit. The man recovers and his career goes on uninterrupted. It's not fair, but it is still reality, even in 2021.

Is the relationship worth risking your career? If the answer for you is yes, go ahead. Remember, being Singlish means telling yourself the truth. Go in with your eyes open to the risks, and with an exit strategy in case it all goes wrong.

In all honesty, the Singlish woman may even be involved in extra-marital affairs. And no, she's not doing it to find someone else to support her. In fact, it's the opposite. The wife of a man who is also seeing a Singlish woman certainly has to examine the state of her marriage, and whether she wants to maintain it, but the truly Singlish woman is probably not the one who will make him walk away from the marital home.

"Getting" the husband may be the last thing the Singlish woman wants. She is honest with herself about the pros and cons, the risks and potential outcomes of being a mistress. She decides whether to go forward with the relationship based on how that fits her life plan. The Singlish woman always tells herself the truth, even in love.

If you do choose to be a mistress, and want to take your lover from his wife, I am not here to judge you. I do, however, recommend that you remember the famous quote, variously attributed to the billionaire Sir James Goldsmith, or to the French actor Sacha Guitry: "A man who marries his mistress creates a vacancy." You already know that he will roam; don't be blind to the possibility that he might roam away from you.

Brenda and Roger: An Office Romance

Brenda, 35, is an event planner. Last year, she met a senior executive from another department while planning a major customer event. They had a lot in common and enjoyed working together. After the last guest left at the end of the big night, they went for a celebratory drink and the executive, Roger, said that he would like to get to know her better. Brenda was interested, but worried about being involved with someone at work. She also thought he had a serious girlfriend, and she wasn't sure how to handle that.

Before we go on, take a minute to think about how you would handle this situation. In my eyes, there is no absolutely right or wrong answer here. There is only what is right for you. What do you think about office romances? What questions do you have? How would you get the answers you need to make a decision? Brenda had questions too; let's see what she did.

Brenda thought about this for a long time. Roger told her that he did have a long-term girlfriend, but things hadn't been going well and they were breaking up. Roger said that Brenda made him happy and optimistic about the future in ways that he hadn't felt in a long time.

Brenda decided to give the relationship a try. For about a year it all went well. They were very discreet at work, and because they worked in different departments, they didn't see each other much during the day. They had dinner and sex about once a week (Roger told his girlfriend he was working late). At big conferences, they would add a day or two to their trip and explore the town.

Roger kept telling Brenda that his relationship with his girlfriend was in serious trouble, but that he couldn't just walk out on her after all their time together. After a while Brenda doubted that he meant it. When she brought it up, the conversation always ended badly. Finally, Brenda broke things off. Although she didn't see Roger often in the office, it was still awkward. In the end, Brenda felt she had to leave. It took 6 months for her to find another job, which she likes as much as her old one.

If the office isn't a good hunting ground, where else can a Singlish woman look for dates?

Many people recommend your house of worship. That assumes that you have one. I don't, and don't want someone religious, so that option is out for me. But if it fits you, try it. Sometimes congregations have singles' groups, with different activities where people can meet. Many of these groups assume that you want marriage, so make sure your expectations match those of the people you are likely to meet. Like any small group, these can also be hothouses for gossip, so be prepared for that, too.

Get involved in other activities that interest you. Many of you will be anyway, since we Singlish women get involved in activities we enjoy. If you like to bike, join a bike club. Ski or snowboard fanatic? Join your local group. Gardener? Find a garden club or community garden. Take a course, join a club, learn something new; there are lots of opportunities. If you don't meet a new man, you might make a good friend.

And then there is the internet: blessing and curse of twenty-first century dating. I've tried several sites in different countries during my "it would be nice to be dating" phases. I've even had one or two decent dates, amongst the duds. I've found that it's far too easy, and too common, for men to lie on their profiles. Do they really think I don't notice that their picture is from 10 years and 50 pounds ago?

Some men seem to think that any woman on a dating app is fair game for cheesy pickup lines. When you say 'no thanks' they get insulted. Develop a thick skin, and if something seems off, swipe him away. You are not obligated to meet, or even talk with, every man who contacts you.

As with so many experiences in life, you never really know what you are getting into until you get there. When you do agree to a date, go with a clear idea of what you are looking for. Bring your sense of humor. Even if the date is so bad that you feign illness and leave early, it's only a few hours. At least you'll have a good story to share with your friends!

Beyond work, social groups and dating apps, remember your existing circle. Tell your good friends what you are looking for. Work the network!

If it takes a while, stay calm. The good ones are worth waiting for. You already know that you can live a fulfilling, interesting life as a single woman. You are a catch! Stay picky, don't compromise on areas that are really important to you, and keep on enjoying your Singlish life.

Dos and Don'ts for Singlish Dating

When and if you do decide to meet one of these dates, wherever you meet him, keep your Singlish self handy. That means maintaining your self-respect at all times. If he's rude, leave. If he's nice enough but you don't really want to see him again, be kind enough to both of you to say so politely. And if you do want to see him again, say that, and even invite him to do something of your choosing. Remember, being Singlish means that you take control of your own life and your own decisions.

One of those important decisions is "how far" to go. Is it OK to have sex on the first, second, third, date? It's your choice, and depends on what you are looking for. I'm pretty slow about these things; for me, attraction is definitely between the ears. I need to know a man pretty well to find him sexy. That doesn't mean that I don't enjoy looking at a nice set of abs on a movie star, but he'd have to put on his shirt and talk with me for a few dates before I did anything about it.

If you are looking for a physical relationship, you will make different decisions. As long as they are your decisions, it's all good. If they are his decisions, that's rape. Report him to the police, see that the charges go through, get help to recover, and move on. You are still Singlish, still strong.

One very serious point to remember: take responsibility for your own safety. I think the first few dates should be in public places. Make sure at least one friend knows where you are and what the plan is. Arrive on your own. I normally leave on my own too: after this long without sex, I know I can wait a little longer. Most importantly, keep your radar on and listen to it. While most men are perfectly safe, there are unfortunately some dangerous ones out there. Listen to your intuition, not your ovaries. If you are uncomfortable, leave. And be sure he's not following you home.

Sad but true, we have to think about these things. The Singlish woman acknowledges the risk, faces her fears, takes appropriate precautions and goes out on dates anyway.

Even the best relationships take attention and effort to get better and to last. Being or becoming

Singlish can help you face issues in a relationship. A man accustomed to making all the decisions without being questioned may not like that a Singlish woman makes decisions for herself. He may get angry or upset, or may just be confused. If you have become Singlish while with him, he might feel that he doesn't know you anymore.

There is no one right answer for what to do in this situation. Decide for yourself what will make you happy and then try to make it happen. If you think he can adjust and you want to stay with him, I encourage you to work on your relationship. Try talking together, and get help from a professional counselor if you need it. Give him a chance to appreciate who you have become.

Whatever happens, hold onto your Singlish principles. You are making these changes because they are right for you. Don't let him talk you out of it.

Fiona: A New Life On Her Own

After 20 years of marriage Fiona, 45, realized that her husband Markus didn't respect her. He treated her like a junior partner in their marriage. He wasn't abusive, and her life met her material needs, but it wasn't enough. Fiona wanted more, and she knew she might have to divorce Markus to be happy.
Leaving a secure marriage was the most frightening thing that Fiona had ever done.

She did it in a very Singlish way. First, she told Markus that she wasn't happy and they both needed to make changes. Markus agreed to try, but he didn't seem to be able to make the changes she was asking for.

While this was happening, Fiona looked at her skills and financial situation, and figured out what income she needed to live as she wanted to. She took some refresher courses to bring her accounting skills up to current standards.

After a few months, Fiona found an entry level role as a bookkeeper for a small business. It didn't pay much, but it gave her confidence and connections, and current work on her CV. She also saw that things with Markus weren't going to improve, and decided to leave him. In 6 months of working, she had saved enough money for the down payment on a small flat. Work provided enough to cover her costs if she watched her money carefully.

Fiona moved out on a Friday, with help from family and friends. On Monday she visited a lawyer and started her divorce. One year later, Fiona is happy with her life; her only regret is that she waited so long to take control of her life. Yes, she has given up monthly spa visits but she is a happier, more fulfilled woman. For her, that's more important.

If, at any point, you think that the work is not worth the relationship, be truthful with yourself. Accept that this is not the right man for you right now. Make your plans and leave. Do it for yourself. You're Singlish; you have the skills and the attitude to make it on your own. You are not trapped.

Successful Singlish Romance

What does a successful Singlish relationship really look like in practice? There are as many kinds of successful Singlish relationships as there are Singlish women. The common thread is that the Singlish woman knows that the relationship is only one part of her life. She is a complete, confident and competent woman beyond it, too.

Here are some examples, drawn from my own or my friends' lives.

Julia's New Man

Julia is a 35-year-old sales representative living in a suburb. She has had some long-term relationships since graduating from university; the last ended 3 years ago. Since then, Julia joined a local hiking club and has taken 2 or 3 weekend trips each year. She also takes herself on at least one warm weather or spa holiday each year, sometimes with friends, sometimes alone.
About 6 months ago, Julia met Steve when he moved into her neighborhood. It wasn't

planned; his dog escaped into her yard while the movers were unloading his furniture. To thank her for keeping his dog safe, Steve invited Julia for coffee and they met at the local coffee shop. During the 2-hour conversation, they discovered several common interests. Steve asked Julia out for dinner the following night. She already had plans, so they picked another day. Now they usually see each other one night during the week and do something together most weekends – sometimes with his or her friends, sometimes just the two of them. Julia keeps some weekends for herself, for a hiking club event or to do something with her friends. Julia's life is a balance between independence and togetherness that fits her needs.

<u>Valerie and Martin</u>

Valerie is a Certified Nurse Practitioner. At 28, she had a full life, and was looking for a man who shared her wish for marriage and children. Valerie met Martin at the local garden club, planting flowers in a vacant lot in their neighborhood. They found that they had a lot in common and began dating. Martin admired Valerie's independence and the fact that she came to the planting session alone, without knowing any of the members, because the vacant lot really bothered her.
Two years later they married, and Valerie is now pregnant with their first child, a girl. She

and Martin have shared friends, and friends they see without one another, and they have a large vegetable garden. Valerie plans to return to work after the baby is born. She wants her daughter to have an independent female role model as well as parents who love and respect one another.

Valerie was Singlish before she married: she looked after herself, pursued her own interests and kept in touch with her own friends. After marriage, she is still Singlish, and is determined to give her daughter the same inner strength and confidence that she has herself.

Because Living Singlish is an attitude you carry within, you can be Singlish whether you are single, married, or dating. It's up to you. Keep the 7 Singlish Principles in mind, and live the life that you want to live. If that includes a partner or spouse, wonderful. If it means keeping your freedom, your life will be just as full and interesting.

Lizzie: I guess I haven't been great about telling myself the truth in my relationships; I kept thinking that David would change and start paying attention to me. It took me a year to get angry enough to break up with him.

Elizabeth: Yes, I remember David. He just wasn't the right guy at that time. You're over him now though, right?

Lizzie: Oh yes, I don't think about him at all.

Elizabeth: Good for you. Do you know what you want for romance now?

Lizzie: Well, as I said, I am not really looking for romance at all just now. Life is complicated enough. I need to think about finding a job, where to live, being on my own — so many things! Is that weird?

Elizabeth: that's not weird at all. It sounds pretty smart to me. When the time comes that you want a boyfriend, just remember the important points we talked about.

Lizzie: I have to know what I want in a boyfriend, and what I won't put up with. If the man is not the right fit, I need to say so and just move on. No more Davids.

Elizabeth: Absolutely right.

Key Singlish Principles About Romance And Relationships

- Have fun! Look for dates with common interests, and who you enjoy spending time with. Dating shouldn't be a chore.
- Know what you want and what you won't put up with. When you date, do it the Singlish way.
- Tell yourself the truth about your romances, even if it is hard to take. If you know he's the wrong guy, for whatever reason, don't hide from it. Face it, break up, and move on.

Looking Singlish: Presence and Style

Lizzie and Elizabeth are deep in conversation. Now they are looking at other people in the cafe, and Lizzie is showing Elizabeth something in a fashion magazine. What are they talking about? Let's listen in…

Lizzie: Why is it that some people always seem to look so perfect? Look at the women at that table by the window. Their hair, clothes, and makeup all seem to work together. I mean, look at you - not only is your outfit great, but it fits your personality. When you walked into this restaurant, people noticed and smiled at you. You even made them seat us at a better table, and you did it so calmly. How did you learn that?

I always have to think about what clothes go together, and I hate speaking in public, though people tell me I am OK at it. I just get embarrassed so easily!

Elizabeth: Don't be so hard on yourself! Remember, I am inside you, you just haven't let me out yet. What you are talking about is presence and style.

Lizzie: Presence and style. What's the difference and how do I get them?

Elizabeth: Style is your own way of looking and acting, Presence is the impact it makes. Give yourself a little time for your tastes to develop. They will change as you get older, though I think you already know what you are comfortable wearing. Our clothes aren't that different: jeans, sweaters, and boots. You are dressed appropriately for a day like today.

You really just build on what you already know, following a few basic principles: know who you are and who you are not; don't try to look just like anyone else.

Don't be afraid to try a new style, gesture, or way of speaking, if it's consistent with who you are.

And celebrate your successes; if someone complements you on your public speaking, say thank you and believe them. Allow yourself to enjoy the complement.

I made some pretty odd choices until I figured it out. You should have seen the outfit I wore when...

When people look at a Singlish woman, what do they see? Impressions form in milliseconds, even before you start to speak. People make snap decisions about your competence, and how likeable or trustworthy you are, as well as whether you are attractive. The decisions are made so quickly that we don't even realize we are making them. More than half of the impression you make on other people is through your body language and other types of non-verbal communication. How you speak, while important, is in no way the whole story. How you dress and hold yourself really does matter.

The Singlish woman has a look that's all her own. It includes her innate presence and her chosen style. Together they show the world that she is a confident, capable woman.

Presence

What is "presence"?

Webster's online dictionary defines presence as "the bearing, carriage, or air of a person; especially: stately or distinguished bearing" or "a noteworthy quality of poise and effectiveness."

I like the phrase "noteworthy quality of poise" quite a lot. Think of presence as the way your internal self shows to the world. It's about how much metaphorical space you take up, regardless of your physical size. A woman with presence will be seen as strong and worth listening to. Best of all, much of your presence comes from within, so it's completely independent of how much money you have to spend on clothes.

Presence includes several factors:

- Posture
- Movements; walk and gestures
- Voice and word choices
- Poise
- Style

When I think about a woman with presence, I think of Christine Lagarde, Managing Director of the International Monetary Fund from 2011-2019, and then President of the European Central Bank. She has a powerful presence, and a style all her own. She never seems flustered, stands tall, speaks calmly and with authority, and somehow you know that she has never allowed herself to be pushed to the side of the room.

What other women can you think of who have this quality? Other women that come to my mind are actress Dame Helen Mirren and journalist Christiane Amanpour. Whenever I see them, they seem to be completely in control of their surroundings, and to be comfortable with who they are. I would never mistake them for anyone else.

I've had teachers like this too. No matter what happened in the classroom, they were always on top of it. You probably know at least one woman like this in your life. Take a minute to think of her, and why she seems to have this quality.

Now let's look at each of the factors that make up presence individually.

Posture

Start by looking at yourself in the mirror, in your normal standing or sitting pose. What impression are you giving?

Standing up straight is perhaps the easiest and hardest thing you can do to improve your presence. Easy because it's something we can all inherently do, but hard because it requires a bit of effort. When you have been standing for a while, or sitting in an uncomfortable chair, it's easy to slump, hunch your shoulders, or stand with one leg bent or a hip stuck out to the side. These might be appropriate in very casual situations, but most of the time you need to stand up straight if you want to be noticed and respected for the Singlish woman you are. Hunching and slumping make you look small and less important.

Nick Morgan, in his book Power Cues,[33] describes 3 basic postures: The Head Posture, The Pelvis Thrust Forward Posture, and the Heart Posture. A woman in the Head Posture has her head tipped forward and eyes down. It makes her look subordinate, weak, defensive and reluctant to be there.

It's hard to project a strong image from this posture. Try it now: tip your chin and shoulders down, look at the floor, and try to say "I am a strong Singlish woman" in a powerful voice. It's difficult. Slumping not only looks bad, but it makes it nearly impossible to speak loudly. Your lungs can't expand to their full capacity, and the air doesn't flow easily.

Women wearing very high heels frequently take on The Pelvis Thrust Forward Posture: the shoes can make you stick your hips forward like a model, just for balance. That's an inherently flirtatious posture – not one in which a woman will be taken seriously. The Singlish woman knows that there is a time for both, and she doesn't flirt when it's not appropriate. Knowing her own high worth, she doesn't need to approach the world that way.

I love high heels as much as (or maybe more than) the next woman, but I have had to change the shoes I wear to work to avoid falling into this trap. My work shoes now have heels no more than about 2 inches (5 cm) high, and while the heels are graceful, they are more solid than stiletto. I have found that people take me more seriously. And yes, other women still complement my shoes.

The third posture, and the one that automatically adds to a woman's presence, is the Heart Posture. This is the one Mom told us to take – head up, shoulders back, and stomach in. Your eyes are open and you engage with the people around you. The Heart Posture projects trustworthiness and confidence. That's how a Singlish woman faces the world!

The same thing works sitting down. If you slump in your chair, people can easily ignore you. Women have to work especially hard to be heard in meetings, so use every tool at your disposal. Sit upright, lean forward into the table slightly, and look people in the eye. Suddenly you are part of the conversation in a way that you can never be if you are looking down or hunched over your phone or computer.

Sit up, sit forward, and look at the people you are talking with. They are more likely to listen to you as an equal. Amazing, and amazingly simple.

Posture is particularly important if, like me, you are on the petite side. I'm 5 feet tall, about 150 cm. If I sit back in a man-sized boardroom chair, my feet don't touch the ground. That definitely undermines my sense of presence.

As you become Singlish, think about these postures. Train yourself to stay in the Heart Posture. As your Singlish self emerges, it will become more natural, and your presence will increase.

Movements: walk and gestures

How you move also affects the way people see you. Actions and gestures can say a lot about your energy, your confidence, and your competence.

For example, what is a strong walk? Stand up straight with your shoulders back and your head up. Look where you are going (not at the floor or your smartphone). Take long firm strides and point your toes straight ahead. Let your arms swing naturally; don't wave them around or pin them stiffly to your sides. That's the walk of a confident Singlish woman.

A woman who always walks right next to the wall, takes short, mincing steps, turns her feet in or out to maintain balance in her high heels, avoids eye contact, or holds her arms still as if they are tied to her sides looks like a woman with no confidence in herself. Why would anyone else have confidence in her abilities? As a Singlish woman, you know that you are capable of great things. Let it show in your walk.

Gestures work the same way. A woman who frequently twirls her hair around her fingers will not be taken as seriously. A woman who tilts her head far to one side when listening to someone else speak is sending unconscious signals that she is subservient, not confident.

Your gestures can make a big difference. I once interviewed a woman for a leadership role. She was a very strong candidate and seemed to have great presence. Then I asked her about a mistake she had made in the past, and what she had learned from it. She put her face in her hands to think. Image ruined! She looked like a little girl caught stealing cookies.

Pay attention to what your hands do when you speak, and what your nervous habits are. Do you tap your fingers? Click your pen? Jiggle your leg up and down? Fiddle with your hair? All of these movements send messages about who you are and what you are like.

If you don't like the impression you make, change it. Find another way to drain off nervous energy or impatience: a deep breath, a word to yourself that helps calm you, a motion no one can see...I sometimes literally bite my tongue in meetings that I think are going too slowly, because no one can see it. Before that, my impatience showed on my face with scowls and sighs. Not the image of someone in control!

The gestures you use to emphasize your statements also matter. How widely and quickly your hands move around sends signals about your self-control and confidence, just like your stride and your posture. Making this a bit more difficult, different cultures are used to different amounts of motion; an Italian, or a New Yorker like me, tends to use bigger gestures more frequently than, for example, a Norwegian. In conservative industries, a senior manager is expected to show more reserve and self-control in her gestures. Yes, it's a bit of a stereotype, but some aspects of culture are not yet universal.

Know your audience and know yourself. What gestures do you make? Do you point at people? Tap the table for emphasis? Wave your arms broadly? Hold them in your lap? When speaking publicly, gestures should be no more than what you need to make your point.

Unless you are on stage and speaking to a large crowd, try to keep your hand gestures in a box in front of your body, and just a little bit wider than your shoulders. Remember not to hold your hands together down below your waist; this is sometimes called the "fig leaf" posture and it closes your posture down. Even worse is the "fig leaf with pen!"

Like changing your posture, changing your gestures can quickly change the impression you make. Watch the people around you, watch yourself, and try new gestures. Watch how people respond. Make more changes if you need to. Again, I like to watch Christine LaGarde for this, or Angela Merkel. I watch politicians from all countries; many of them have been trained in how to use gestures when speaking. Even if I don't understand their words, I can learn a lot from their body language.

If you want to be respected and taken seriously, walk like you know where you are going, and make deliberate hand and arm motions. These simple behavior changes can quickly increase your presence.

Voice and word choices

Some women are born with strong voices. From early childhood they speak clearly, loudly, and in the middle registers of pitch. It's easy to understand them, and their voices seem to give them innate authority.

The rest of us must think about how we sound. If you have a naturally quiet, breathy, or high-pitched voice it's easier for others to see you as childlike, rather than as a strong, competent woman.

How strong is your natural speaking voice? Think about how you speak with your family or very close friends. What tones, pitches and volume come to you naturally? If you sound more confident with them than in the office or with strangers, take heart. That strong voice is your natural one; you just have to practice using it in less familiar or less comfortable situations.

Start with small meetings of close colleagues or strike up conversations with strangers at the coffee shop to practice using that stronger voice in public. Each time you do it, even for just 5 minutes, congratulate yourself. You have taken a step towards increasing your presence.

If your voice tends to be light, quiet, or breathy with close friends, it's time for a decision. You can try to change it on your own; again, practice here is the key. You can get help from a professional voice coach or advice from a friend with a stronger voice. Or you can choose to keep your voice as it is, and work with the other aspects of presence to bring out your Singlish self. You may have to be twice as deliberate when choosing your tones and gestures to get others to take you more seriously and respect your decisions. But if that's what you prefer, do it. Remember, it's not about what I think is right; it's about doing what you know is right for you.

Words, on the other hand, are easy to change. We choose what words come out of our mouths every day. To make a difference in your presence with words, speak calmly and deliberately. Avoid curses, "trendy" words and fillers like um, uh, and like (as in, like, extra words that like, don't, you know, add anything to the meaning). Any word overused becomes a filler: actually, really, to make a long story short…all of these imply that you aren't confident about your statements. The Singlish woman is confident, knows her mind and sticks by her decisions. She takes these insecure-sounding words out of her speech.

Compare these two women speaking to a manager about their business idea:

Woman 1: I really would like to um, tell you about this idea I had. I think it could sort of be a good thing for us to try, you know?

Woman 2: My idea will increase our sales by at least 5% per customer, with no additional sales rep time needed. Let me tell you about the details.

What picture do you have in your mind of each of these women?

I picture Woman 1 standing in front of the boss's desk like a schoolchild, looking down, grasping her notebook tightly and hoping that her boss will somehow ask her to tell him more.

I see Woman 2 walking with her boss on the way to an important meeting, with her head up, taking long strides. She turns to look her boss in the eye for the second sentence, knowing that she has his full attention.

Now, be honest with yourself. In which situations do you sound like Woman 1, and in which ones do you sound like Woman 2? In what ways do you sound like Woman 1 or Woman 2?

If you are not happy with the answers, it's time to think about making a change. Start by thinking about the parts you are good at. Give yourself credit for these and appreciate them. They are the foundation on which you will build.

Here's an easy exercise to help you reduce your fillers. For one day, listen to yourself talk, and figure out what your filler word or phrase is. The next day, write down the number of times you use it. Each week, try to reduce the number of times by 10%; keep track to see your progress. You will automatically sound more knowledgeable and confident, and your inner confidence when speaking will grow. Use the 10% reduction as a goal and celebrate each time you reach it.

Poise

Poise is the ability to keep your cool when everyone around you is losing theirs. A woman with poise gives people the impression that she is completely in control of the situation, even if the bathroom is flooded, the neighbor's kids just threw a ball through her window, the cat missed the litter box, and she's late for work. It's fine to feel overwhelmed by all of these things happening at once; just don't let others know that you feel that way.

A friend of mine who had great poise in the office used to say, "professionals make it look easy." I thought about that a lot as I was moving up the company ladder and tried to live it.

How do you show poise? Start by staying calm when others are getting upset. Take a breath and think before you speak, then speak calmly and deliberately. Resist the temptation to speak more quickly, or with more superlatives (or expletives!) when the pressure mounts.

Yes, some emergencies may require instant action. But outside of hospitals, accident scenes, crimes in progress and natural disasters these are pretty rare. Most crises will benefit from a few minutes of deliberate thinking and planning before you respond. Even if your heart is racing, don't let on how stressed you are.

In crises, people who show their stress are heard, but people who appear calm are listened to. If you can appear calm to others when they are stressed, you are showing poise. Congratulate yourself for that, no matter what the outcome of the crisis turns out to be.

The same is true in stressful situations that don't involve a major crisis. For some people, giving presentations is enough to make them weak at the knees. For others, it's not the presenting, but the questions afterwards that cause them to lose their composure. Whatever makes you nervous, identify it and find ways to practice. Give your big presentation in front of friends and family to get used to seeing people react (you should be rehearsing it anyway, to become completely comfortable with the flow). Have friends or colleagues challenge your ideas so that you can rehearse answers to tough questions. Anticipating challenges and knowing your answers ahead of time, goes a long way in helping you stay cool under pressure.

The best part of poise is that the more crises you handle, the more successes you celebrate for yourself, the more confidence you will have. And confidence increases poise.

Stylish and Singlish

Every woman has her own personal style, which is different from every other woman's, even if they wear the same clothes. How the clothes fit, how you combine them, what accessories you wear all contribute to making you look completely different from any other woman in the same outfit. This is something that you have that no one else can copy. The Singlish woman knows her style and makes the most of it.

Style includes your clothes, shoes, jewellery, handbags, glasses, hairstyle, even your car and your mobile phone case. It also includes how you wear them: how many buttons on that blouse do you leave open? Do you wear several necklaces at once, just one, or none at all? Do you push your glasses onto your head when not using them, keep them on a chain, or take them off? These are all things that you choose, and all of the choices contribute to your style.

Many female celebrities become known for their particular style. Jacqueline Kennedy, Michelle Obama, Madonna, Victoria Beckham, Kim Kardashian…whether or not you like their styles, you recognize them as reflections of each woman's unique personality.

Your personal style can evolve over time. Look at the clothes you wore and how you wore them five or more years ago. You will probably see a difference from how you dress today. It might be in your clothes, accessories, or hairstyle. Your personal style should reflect who you are at that point in time, including both the core aspects of your personality, and those that change. Madonna and Christina Aguilera are good examples. Whether in fishnet, leather or designer suits, all of their outfits are clearly their own.

You already have the basics of your own style within you. As a Singlish woman, you know what you like and what you don't like, what catches your eye and what leaves you bored. That's the foundation of your style. Add in what's appropriate for your age and occupation and you are well on your way.

When choosing clothes, think about the image you want to project. What's appropriate? To be taken seriously in the conservative business world, avoid deep V-necks that emphasize your cleavage. The same goes for open-toed shoes and sandals. They can be very attractive. They just don't belong in most corporate environments. Do you want people to recognize you as a free spirit? Wear brighter colors, maybe something looser and more flowing.

The idea is not to wear what I tell you to wear, but to wear what feels right for you and furthers the image you want to project. When you look in the mirror, you should recognize the Singlish woman looking back at you.

Makeup works the same way. You've probably seen pictures of celebrities with and without makeup, or run into someone you know in that situation, and thought, "wow, what a difference!" To me, makeup shouldn't change who you are. At its best, it can subtly emphasize certain parts or help you make a particular impression.

Selina: Dressing for Work and Fun

Selina, 28, works in an investment bank. During the day, she wears a conservative pantsuit, closed-toe shoes with moderate heels, and light makeup in natural shades. She might wear a brightly colored scarf or pin to liven it up a bit. If Selina worked in a more creative environment, like an advertising agency, she might wear bright colors and flowing tops, and might add a statement necklace. She dresses according to what is appropriate for her company and her clients.

When Selina goes dancing with friends, she looks very different: higher heels, big jewellery, a sparkly shirt or skirt, bright lipstick and colorful eye shadows. Again, her outfit is appropriate for what she is doing. Both are recognizably her style, not anyone else's.

Hair is an important part of your style, too. Because it's near your face, people look at it. And for some reason, people feel free to comment on it. So think about your hairstyle. Different lengths and types of cuts go better with certain facial shapes. Some people prefer longer hair, and some prefer shorter.

If you are a free spirited, creative person, longer hair with a shaggier cut might appeal to you. If you are more self-contained, you might prefer shorter hair, or longer hair done up in a bun. Do you color your hair? What color? It's all part of your style.

In many cultures, pigtails and side braids are only for by little girls. Wearing your hair this way will imply that you are young or inexperienced. Think hard before you make it part of your professional look.

Choose your accessories the same way. Some women develop a signature piece. Madeline Albright, the former US ambassador to the United

Nations and US Secretary of State, was known for her brooches, which she often chose to send a message or make a point. She even published a book about them in 2009, called Read My Pins: Stories from a Diplomat's Jewel Box.

What about tattoos? Tattoos are increasingly common and visible. Some are truly beautiful pieces of body art. If you want to get a tattoo, go ahead and do it. Just remember that it is permanent and think about the implications for your career and the rest of your life.

You may find yourself in situations where tattoos are not appropriate. In many industries, tattoos (and piercings) are not approved of. Where is your tattoo? Will you be able to cover it up if you have to? If you have tattoos on your arms, are you comfortable with the idea of always wearing long sleeves to work? It's your choice; think first, then decide.

Basic Singlish Style Tips

We've seen that style is an important part of your presence. What do you do if you aren't sure about yours? Here are some simple ways to start building and maintaining your own unique Singlish style:

Learn how to dress for your body type and natural coloring. Each of us has a shape to our bodies. The four most common are hourglass, apple, pear and rectangle. Each shape looks better in different types of clothes. A woman with one shape can look terrible in clothes that are perfect for a woman with another. The same is true for hair and complexion; these drive the colors we look good in. Some women look better in "warm" rich tones. Others look better in cooler, paler tones or even pastels and white.

Choose clothes and accessories that look best with your shape and complexion. I have an hourglass shape, pale skin and dark hair. If I wear a high-waisted pale-yellow dress, I look terrible. But if I wear jewel-toned outfits that accentuate my waist, I look vibrant and healthy. One of my close friends is also an hourglass but has paler skin and darker hair than I do. She looks fabulous in orange and wears it as a main color or accent almost every day. I would look terrible.

For advice on style and makeup, get a consultation at a reputable shop, or look online or in fashion magazine for tips. If you wear makeup, take advantage of the consultations in stores. You do not have to use all of their suggestions, and you don't have to buy anything unless you want to. You can just benefit from the advice. Find what works for you and fits your Singlish look, then stick with it. You can make modifications to keep yourself looking on trend while sticking with your own personal look and style.

Your style should be consistent with who you know yourself to be, and with the image you want to project.

Working on your presence not only makes you look more confident to yourself, it makes other people have confidence in you too. Find someone whose posture, gestures or manner of speaking, poise, or style you admire, and watch them closely. It could be a colleague, professor, politician, or even a neighbor. Try out some of their moves, then incorporate them into your own, unique, Singlish presence. While it can feel like acting at the beginning, it's really about letting your Singlish presence shine through.

Ultimately Singlish presence comes from inner confidence, from knowing that you can support yourself, make your own decisions and manage your own life. Feeling good about your Singlish state will show, and will increase your presence without any extra work from you.

Elizabeth: So you see, clothing is only part of style and presence.
Lizzie: I understand. How I dress needs to match the way I talk, my posture, how I move, and how I react in different situations. It should all feel like 'me.' If I am not being true to myself, it will show.
Elizabeth: Exactly right.
Lizzie: So I have to be very clear about who I am and not try to be anyone else. I need to be a little more honest when I

look in the mirror. I have some clothes that look much better on my best friend than they do on me. And sometimes I slouch instead of standing up – especially if I feel unsure. When I catch myself doing that, or saying 'like' too much, I need to stop.

Elizabeth: Yes, you can do all of that. What about when you catch yourself getting it right? What should you do when you get through a tough conversation well, or use very appropriate tones and gestures in when giving a presentation?

Lizzie: I need to congratulate myself and celebrate it.

Singlish Principles for Presence and Style

- Know who you are, and who you are not. Be yourself and let your look speak for itself. The more comfortable you become with how you look and who you are, the more natural presence you will have.
- Tell yourself the truth about what looks good, and whether the image you project now matches the one you want to project.
- Try a new style, posture, or way of speaking that shows your inner Singlish self.
- Celebrate your successes. When someone complements your poise or look, say thank you and allow yourself to enjoy their comment.

The Singlish Woman Works

Back in the cafe, the discussion is turning serious. Lizzie is asking lots of questions and she's just pulled out a pad to take notes. What are they talking about now?

Lizzie: All of this is good information, but what I really worry about is working and money. How do I get a job?

How will I know that I can do it? How do I get promoted? What if I work with people I don't like? What is it like to work on the same schedule every day? At school I can arrange not to have any early classes on Mondays, but I can't do that at work, right? I have so many questions and I feel kind of silly asking them.

Elizabeth: This is a really important topic and I am glad that you brought it up. We could spend days talking about work. Lots of people have these questions. Very few people know exactly what they want to do or whether they will like it. Let's start with basics.

Lizzie: With graduation coming closer and no job yet, this keeps me up at night.

Elizabeth: Well, having a good career is really important. You won't suddenly inherit a fortune when you graduate, and you don't want to be dependent on anyone. Work is what makes that possible. We need to talk about what behaviors can help or hurt your career, how to interact with your colleagues, and what it is really like to be a woman in the workplace.

Lizzie: I think you are going to tell me about a few principles I need to follow, right?

Elizabeth: Right! Important ones here are knowing what you do and do not want, having the discipline to stick by your decisions, trying new things, and celebrating your successes. Your career is your responsibility. No one knows what you want from it better than you do. My friends and I had to learn some hard lessons along the way. Let's see if we can make it easier for you. Would you like to know what my first few days at my first job were like?

Lizzie: Yes, please.

Elizabeth: Ok, you will definitely be able to do better than I did...

Unless you had the good luck to be born to extraordinarily wealthy and generous parents, or you have won the lottery, work will be part of your Singlish life. That's good, actually. Work gives us the opportunity to grow, to stretch, to meet people, and gives us choices.

There are a host of books telling you how to pick your career, how to find a job or career you love, or how to start a business, if you are so inclined. In this book, we'll look at how Singlish women think about work.

You can be Singlish with any job or career; it just needs to give you financial freedom, so you don't have to rely on anyone else for money. The best jobs also give you a sense of accomplishment and satisfaction. You'll learn and do more than you think possible.

These benefits can come from any job. As trite as this sounds, it's not about the job level, the amount of money or a prestigious title. Any job can be a Singlish woman's job. The Singlish woman knows that her worth comes from what she thinks of herself, and the value she places on her contributions. It doesn't come from anyone else's opinion, any more than other people's opinion of her romantic life determines her own satisfaction with it.

Equally as important, your job is not your life. You can change jobs. It may take time to find another job, but you can do it. Being Singlish gives you the skills and confidence to make the decisions that will help you get this right.

Keep that in mind at work. You are choosing to do this, and you could just as easily choose to do something else. That's true even if you think you are unskilled; balancing the details of your life against getting to work every day already means that you are motivated, organized, and capable.

You can change your career along the way, too. I'm definitely not doing what I planned to do as a child! My own career trajectory started with veterinary practice, which had been my dream since childhood. After 5 years, allergies drove me out of practice, and I moved to a company that made medicines for animals. I worked my way up to the Executive Committee in a technical function, dropped down to move into Marketing, and began fighting my way back up again. The company was bought, and I didn't see any opportunities in the new one, so I took the severance package and walked to write this book.

Later I returned to the company in another department and worked there for 3 years before leaving again. I am now deciding what I want to do next. I might go back to a big company, or a small one. I might do something completely different, and focus on my writing. Yes it's a little bit scary. But after years of Singlish living, I am confident of my abilities and have enough savings to give me the freedom to take another "career deep breath."

We're Singlish women, so let's be honest with each other. There are some basic truths about women and work in the twenty-first century that every Singlish woman (every woman, really) should recognize.

The Truth About Single Women and Careers

From my experience, here's the ugly truth about women in business:

- Most business cultures are still set up by or for men. Women are still the "other."
- The pay gap between men and women exists, and won't go away until each woman stands up and demands equal pay for equal work.
- The debate is focusing increasingly on Mommy Track vs. male career track. Single women with careers and lives are not even being discussed. We need to make our expectations clear and stick to them.
- Harassment still exists, no matter how much sensitivity training and how many Diversity and Inclusion programs are put in place.
- The Old Boy's Network still rules. We need to make our own network and support each other (and any worthy men).

- You can't "lead like a woman" (whatever that means) and win. You have to observe at least some of the men's rules, or they will never let you into their club. Doing that, and still being true to yourself, is a minefield.

The truth is, even the strongest, most confident female leaders struggle sometimes. If you don't believe me, listen to some interviews. Powerful women need a circle of support, have moments of doubt, and are asked questions that reporters would never ask a man. When was the last time you heard an interviewer ask a man how he balances work and family, or which designer's clothes he was wearing for the interview? They ask women these questions all the time.

Some of the data coming out now gives new insights into these truths. For example, a landmark paper from McKinsey and Co. [30] showed that any minority must be 30% of a group before they are no longer viewed as "tokens" or outsiders. According to Catalyst, in December 2020 only 6% of CEOs of S&P 500 companies were women.[7] We have a frightfully long way to go.

Getting bitter about this won't change anything. A Singlish woman knows that her satisfaction or dissatisfaction with this state of affairs doesn't really matter to the world. What matters is how she chooses to react. She can choose to try to change the system, to work within it, or to opt out and strike out on her own. It's about the choices she makes, standing on her own two feet. She knows that she can look after herself, and that in the end she will be fine.

Despite the fact that women began entering the corporate workforce in larger numbers in the middle of the last century, we're still often expected to fit old models of ideal behavior. Things have become better over time – it's not quite like "Mad Men" out there anymore – but I am continually amazed when I trip over these old expectations still lying around.

More disturbing, the expectations are held by some men of our own generations: our brothers, cousins and friends. I don't understand it. But I do acknowledge the problem and react accordingly. Singlish women don't hide from the truth. Here are some issues the Singlish woman has to deal with as she earns her way in the world.

Attitudes About Strong Women in the Workplace

It's absolutely critical to know what want from your career and your job. Communicating that, however, can be tricky. Women are still called aggressive and are denigrated, when a man saying the same thing in the same way would be called assertive and be admired.

Even when we make our points quietly and calmly, there is something about a woman persisting in support of her position that seems to trigger these labels. Women who don't figure out how to manage this conundrum will quickly get a reputation as that delightful 5 letter word, the Bitch. (My mother once told me that Bitch meant "Beautiful Intelligent Terrific Charming Human Being." I wore a big silver 'B' around my neck for years after that). Persist anyway.

My company claimed to have a "speak up culture" and encouraged questions. One department head actually did, and I was fortunate to work for him for six years. When I moved to another department where speaking up was not welcome, I was told to be less aggressive and confrontational. The fact is, if you are a woman you will face this and have to find your path through it. Unfortunately, there is no simple answer.

Launching Your Career

In the past, employees (mostly men) joined a company early in life and stayed there until retirement. They were often promoted based on seniority rather than skills. At the end of a 30-year career, they retired with a watch and went off to spoil the grandchildren. Make no mistake, those days are gone. If you want a career, you have to make it happen. Singlish women enjoy this; we love to make the important decisions for ourselves!

It starts with deciding what you want to do. Think about an industry or profession that really interests you. Find out more about it, choose companies that fit your abilities, interests and needs, and apply for jobs there. Your first job in an industry sets the tone for your whole career, so do it right. Go to the interview prepared to talk about your skills and interest and how hiring you will help the company.

Be brave: apply for a job even if you don't think you match it 100% on paper. That's something the boys learn early that we don't. If you have 75%, or even 60% of the skills that the ad says are required, try anyway. You are smart and decisive; you can learn the rest. The men do!

Follow the seventh Singlish Principle and try something new. Work is a great place to develop new skills, so put your hand up and volunteer. Sure, you might make some mistakes. That's not only fine, it's actually one of the best ways to learn. When you make a mistake, think about what went wrong and why. Once you see where you went off track, you'll be able to spot the problem earlier next time and not repeat your error.

Everyday Working Life

Work is not like school; you have to go every day, and they notice if you don't show up. You usually have to adjust to the office schedule and get there at about the same time everyone else does. Since the COVID-19 lockdowns of 2020, more companies allow flexible hours and working from home. Those can be a big help, especially if you have other commitments or a long commute.

One reality check: sometimes company policies and the office culture don't match. Find out whether colleagues resent or look down on people who request an altered schedule before deciding whether you really need that extra hour of sleep in the morning. It might be worth learning to go to sleep an hour earlier instead.

Whether you take advantage of the flexible working policy or not, you have to do more than just show up or log on. Always be there mentally as well as physically. Be friendly and reliable. Reliability means that you are on time and prepared for meetings and you don't miss deadlines.

Turn in quality work, too. If you are not sure of how to do something, don't wait until the deadline to ask for help. Think about how you would feel if you were relying on someone else to give you important information. What would you do if, the day before you needed it, they told you that they had no idea how to get started? You might explode, right? Don't do it to anyone else. You will get a terrible reputation and no opportunities for promotion or interesting projects. You might even find yourself out of a job.

Each workplace has its own culture. Some offices are friendly. People keep their office doors open, stop in to chat, and take coffee breaks and lunch together. Others are much more serious. I've seen offices where everyone's door is closed, people eat at their desks and seem embarrassed to be caught needing a bathroom break. I've seen open spaces where no one has an office that are boisterous and friendly and open spaces where no one dares to say a word.

My friend Daria worked for many years in a friendly office. Team members went out for lunch together, celebrated birthdays with cake, emailed each other jokes and tried to have some fun despite being in a high-pressure department. She moved to another company where no one spoke to anyone else unless absolutely necessary It was hard to believe, but she could go for 3 or 4 days without talking with a colleague, even if that person sat next to her. The norm in that office was to send a (very formal) email if you had even the smallest question. It was a total mismatch for her personality. She left after a year for a company with a friendlier office culture.

Try to get a sense of this during your interview. Ask questions of your interviewers and try to meet some of the people that you would be working with, if that's possible. When you start, go with the flow and try to fit in. Even if it's a total mismatch, it's not a disaster. You're still gaining experience and getting paid. Stay for a year if you can; that's really not as long as you think. Spend that year learning as much as possible, while looking for a job that lets you be truer to yourself. You can do it.

Whatever the culture is, always look and act professionally. Show up. Look presentable. Be reliable. Make sure you get credit when you do the job well, and give others credit for a job well done too. Take responsibility for your mistakes, and take steps to fix them, as you would with any other part of your Singlish life. Work funds your Singlish lifestyle; give it the attention it deserves.

Making and Taking Opportunities

Women still don't get the same opportunities as men. Managers will assume that women are less willing to move, or aren't interested in challenges. We even make it easier for them to think that: many of us believe that if we do our jobs well, the raises and promotions will be given to us. Sheryl Sandberg called it waiting for the tiara floating in the hallway.[38] Here's a free tip: it doesn't exist. If you want the opportunity, the new role, the promotion, or the raise, you have to ask for it.

The book *Women Don't Ask: The High Cost of Avoiding Negotiation, and Positive Strategies for Change*,[1] by Linda Babcock and Sara Laschever, includes some of the most straightforward advice I have ever read on negotiating for money and positions at work. I re-read it about once a year.

The main message is that we, as women, must ask for what we want and deserve, and we need to base our requests on facts. Saying that we worked harder than anyone else isn't enough. We need to use facts about what we have produced, how we have performed, and how that helped the business. Yes, it can feel awkward to push ourselves forward. But we need to do it. If you know what you want, and you are brave enough to ask for it, you might be amazed at what you can get for yourself.

Base your requests on measurable facts that matter. Instead of talking about how hard you work, highlight your accomplishments. Exceeding sales and profit targets, finishing projects on time and on or under budget, and streamlining processes to save time are all concrete achievements that matter to your company. Use them as the centerpiece of your request.

Compare your salary and responsibilities to that of others in your company and industry. While you might not know what your peers in the office earn, you can find out what your peers in other companies make on sites like salary.com and glassdoor.com. If you're underpaid, or working at higher level than your job title indicates, include that in your proposal. As in any negotiation, know what your bottom line is. Be patient, be persistent, and know when it's time to walk away and look for a job somewhere else. Your job fuels your Singlish lifestyle. You deserve to be treated and compensated fairly for what you contribute.

A Singlish attitude gives a woman the skills and confidence to make her own opportunities. It has made it easier for me to seek out and take roles that stretched me, including international assignments, which have allowed me to see parts of the world I never would have expected, which has made me more confident and adaptable, which in turn has led to more international assignments and promotions, which…well, you get the idea.

It's possible for women who are married or otherwise attached to do the same, but the ugly truth is that it is hard on the trailing partner, and many men aren't willing drop their own careers to follow their wives. This is another choice requiring facts, open discussion and awareness of the very real risks and benefits. Whether contemplating a move alone or with a partner or family, think it through and make your decision based on facts. Then go after what you want!

Bernadette's Big Move

Bernadette was an editor at a well-respected magazine, in a city she loved, and where she had lots of friends. She had always wanted to travel abroad but somehow never did. One day she gathered her courage and told her manager, Lorraine, that she wanted to work abroad. Bernadette reminded Lorraine of how she had updated the magazine's layout and improved its digital circulation, comparing that with the magazine's old-fashioned layouts and falling subscription rates in other countries. She asked for the chance to try to turn around one of these sister publications. A year later, Lorraine offered her a 2-year assignment in Paris, at their English-language publication in France.

Bernadette was excited and a little scared. Moving alone to a strange country where she spoke little of the language was intimidating. And there was no job guarantee back home if it didn't work out. Still, Bernadette thought she would try.

After negotiating for language lessons along with her relocation package, she moved to Paris. The first few months were difficult, adjusting to a new culture and to not knowing her way around. With time Bernadette made friends in her neighborhood, learned to navigate the Metro and to buy the best bread at her local boulangerie, and now she loves it. She travels around Europe alone or with friends and has seen more of the world than she had ever imagined possible. Bernadette may not stay in France forever, but she is glad she went.

Work-Life Balance

A hot topic these days, work-life balance (or work-life integration) refers to how much relative time and attention you give you your career vs. the other aspects of your life. The discussion is increasingly about giving time to husbands and children, but it is just as important for single women. Singlish women are particularly prepared to handle this, because they know what is important and can stand by their decisions.

Companies make assumptions about single women, and while you can't stop them, you can control your response. So if anyone expects you to work longer hours because "you have nothing to get home to," and you want to do it, go ahead but (and this is critical!) make sure you are compensated for it, in dollars or opportunities for advancement. And if you don't want to do it, don't hesitate to say, "I have another commitment" (not "I'm sorry..." The Singlish woman doesn't apologize for her decisions). Once you say no, stick with your decision like the strong Singlish woman you are. If you let them push you around once, they'll do it again.

Companies are thrilled to have employees who sacrifice their personal lives for the company's needs. However constant work is not a full life, and the Singlish woman, even with great ambition, knows it. She knows that the balance is not necessarily 50/50, and that there may be short times when she has to sacrifice on one side or the other to have the life she wants. But she makes her decisions based on what's right for her and manages the impact.

I now think of work-life balance as something that applies over the course of my whole life. In the end, I will have worked enough to learn, grow, and achieve the satisfaction of a job well done. But when I retire, I will still have friends and interests that give me another type of satisfaction. That only happens if I nurture those friendships and interests before retirement, so I give them the attention they need now.

Laurie's Life Priorities

Laurie loves her career as a global marketing manager. She was divorced 10 years ago and has 2 grown children. Three years ago, Laurie began volunteering with the local food bank, and it has become an important part of her life. She's now on the food bank's board, and working to increase food security in her city.

Laurie has done well at work; her brands are number 1 and 2 in their markets. Working with her colleagues in different countries is great fun.

Last month Laurie's manager asked her to take a trip that would interfere with the food bank's main annual funding drive. Laurie was already scheduled to speak with the mayor that week; the date could not be changed. She told her manager that, while she was happy to make the trip, she needed to do it at a different time, as she had prior commitments.

Her manager resisted, telling Laurie that she had to put her job first. Laurie held her ground, politely and firmly explaining that she would make the trip the following week, and that she knew that there was no time pressure on the trip. After a bit of conversation, her manager agreed. Laurie stood up for something important to her, and was able to meet both of her obligations.

Sexual Harassment

This is real, still goes on, and takes many forms, from bad jokes and rude comments to flashing in person or during video conferences, unwanted hugs and full-blown physical assault. It's ridiculous and completely unacceptable. It's also reality, and Singlish women deal with reality even while trying to improve things. So here are a few tips, learned over a lifetime on the front lines.

If a man harasses you, remember that you have not done anything wrong. He has. The man who harasses you has crossed a line. He should be uncomfortable, ashamed, and frankly, afraid of the consequences.

Develop a thick skin and a sense of proportion. Some comments should be shrugged off; others can be handled privately. Eleanor Roosevelt, who grew into a true Singlish woman, believed that all women in public life need skin "as tough as a rhinoceros hide." She was consistently attacked in the papers as a Communist, a bad wife and mother, a danger to America…but she learned to ignore it and persevere. We can all learn from her.[12, 13]

If the offense is serious, call out the bad behavior. A simple "that's inappropriate, don't do it again" in a calm, strong voice right after an off-color comment is often enough. If the man is boorish enough to take offense, threaten you, or do it again, escalate the complaint to your manager, the HR department, or a similar authority at work immediately. Don't back down; it's the only way to change their attitude.

If he makes a major move, touching you inappropriately, exposing himself in person or digitally, or threatening you with retaliation, go immediately to the head of HR and the company lawyer. Do not let them talk you out of pursuing this. You have a legal right not to be sexually assaulted at work, and they have a responsibility to give you a safe workplace. Be strong. Go back to my first statement: You did nothing wrong. He did. Remind the company of that if you have to.

Women need to stick together on this. If you have experienced harassment at this company or by this man, other women probably have too. Don't let it happen to anyone else. Fight back. Maintain your sense of yourself and your self-respect.

Office Friendships

Wouldn't it be wonderful if we could find our closest friends at work, the way we did at school? Life would be much easier. But here's the truth, Singlish ladies: Work Is Work. It's not social hour, it's not school and it's not playtime.

While you will meet many people at work get along well with most of them, friendships in the office can be quite different than those outside. They are more about jobs, accomplishments, accountability and, of course, money. If you are climbing a ladder, competition for promotions can disrupt office friendships. Office friendships can be warm and fun, but they are usually not personal in the same way as the friendships you have with people you meet outside of work.

Ideally you will find a job where you can enjoy spending time with and talking with your colleagues, sharing meals and even traveling for business with them. Remember though that work friendships can also be quite political. The most popular people are the ones who can get things done. They either work hard and deliver, or can inspire other people to work hard and deliver for them. It's all about the output. If you let your team down, not only will they not want to have lunch with you, they can damage your reputation and thus your ability to do your job, not to mention your earning power.

That's not to say that you can't find real friends at work. I met several close friends in the office.

But we usually didn't work on the same projects; we met because we worked in the same department, or because we were always taking a coffee break at the same time. We rarely talk about work outside the office. That's how I knew they could be real friends and not just working colleagues; we had a lot more in common than just work.

Even now, when working from home for long periods has become acceptable or even expected, those of us with full-time jobs spend most of our day working or thinking about work. If we do travel to an office, we often think about work during our commute time too. Focus on the job at hand and put 110% of your effort into it while working. When the working day is done, turn your mind and your energy to another part of your life. Make the most of your work time, just as you make the most of your free time.

The Singlish woman thinks consciously about the work she does and does not want to do. She tells herself the truth about whether she is good at her job, whether she enjoys it, and where she wants her career to go. She doesn't confuse her job with her life, or her colleagues with her personal friends. The Singlish woman creates a working life that fits into her larger life, following the Singlish principles.

Nellie Bly

As recently as the early 1900's, having a career was nearly unheard of for women. The journalist Nellie Bly was a pioneer who created her own spectacularly Singlish life in those years. In 1885, she wrote a letter to the Pittsburgh Dispatch newspaper, objecting to a misogynistic column called 'What Girls are Good For.' The author advised women to stay home, because that was all they were capable of doing. Nellie strongly disagreed. The editor was so impressed by her letter that he hired her to work for the Dispatch. That's when she changed her real name, Elizabeth Cochrane, for her pen name, Nellie Bly.
Nellie wanted to do serious reporting, so she moved to Mexico and became a foreign correspondent. Her articles criticizing Mexico's dictatorial government were so pointed that they threatened to arrest her. Although she had to flee back to the US, she kept writing.
Two of her most famous assignments were going undercover as a patient to expose conditions in New York City's notorious Women's Lunatic Asylum on Blackwell's Island, and her solo trip around the world. Her reports of both make fascinating reading, even one hundred years later.
Later Nellie married Robert Seaman, owner of the Iron Clad Manufacturing Company. When

he died, she ran the company, securing several patents in her own name.
Unfortunately, unscrupulous employees embezzled so much money from the Iron Clad Manufacturing Company that it went bankrupt, and Nellie was cast back on her own resources.
Still Singlish despite the setback, Nellie remained strong and returned to reporting. She covered World War One and the American women's suffrage movement.
Nellie Bly, Singlish to the last, died in 1922 at age 57. Throughout her life, she looked after herself, knew what she did and did not want, and pursued her dreams.[4, 5, 44]

Elizabeth: So you see, as important as work is, it's still only one part of your Singlish life. Decide what role you want work to have in your whole existence, then make that happen.

Lizzie: Got it. I can handle the day-to-day bits by following the principles. I need to know what I want and ask for it. I need to stand by my decisions and try new challenges. I need to learn from my mistakes and celebrate my success. And I need to treat my colleagues the way I want to be treated, by being friendly and reliable.

Elizabeth: Yes. We could talk about work for hours, maybe even days. There are so many lessons to share. Work lets you live independently, so it's important to both enjoy it and get it right.

Lizzie: I know. I'm sure that I will ask you about it again. For now, though, could we go on to something else? Talking about work makes me think about money...

Applying Singlish Principles at Work

- Know what you want, and what you don't want. Go after the work that interests you, decline inappropriate assignments and don't let your job overwhelm your life.
- Celebrate your successes. Let people know when you have made a difference, and be proud of what you accomplish.
- Be brave enough to try something new. You don't have to be 110% qualified to apply for a job you want.

Personal Finance

Now Lizzie and Elizabeth are talking about money. Lizzie seems a little bit uncomfortable, while Elizabeth is relaxed.

Elizabeth: I'm proud of you. You are asking all the right questions. It's obvious that you are really thinking about what you want for the future. What else should we talk about?

Lizzie: Well this is a little awkward, but I am really worried about money. I'd like to buy myself nice clothes and go on vacations.

Some of my friends always seem to have a lot of money, and some are always asking me for loans. I don't want to have to ask my friends to buy lunch for me. I don't know where to start. What should I do with my money?

Elizabeth: This is an important question. It's tempting to spend your money as you make it and live for today. I did that for a while, and it was fun. But then I realized if I lived only for today, I would have nothing for tomorrow. You're smart enough to know that doesn't work.

Managing your money requires following 3 principles: Look after yourself by planning for the future, make decisions and stand by them, and be honest with yourself. There are a few terms to learn, and you need a little self-control, but the basics aren't that hard. You don't have to do it all yourself, either. This is one of those areas that benefits from getting knowledgeable advice. Listen to experts, then make the final decisions yourself.

Money. We all need it, we all want it, and most of us have to work to get it. And that's fine. Nothing can match the satisfaction and confidence that comes from knowing that you truly are independent, that you can earn enough to meet your own needs.

Most of us can think of someone we know who had problems because she didn't know how to handle money. Maybe it was the college roommate who paid for 4 years of clothes, vacations and parties on a credit card and is now drowning in debt she can't pay back. Or the old friend who moved in and joined finances with her boyfriend, only to have him move out and take all their money with him. Maybe it was the aunt who let her husband handle all the finances, until he died of a heart attack. She didn't know where their bank records were or whether he had life insurance.

I want you to have the skills and confidence to make the right decisions for your life, so these nightmare scenarios don't happen to you.

Too many girls are afraid of managing their own money. It involves math, decisions, saying no to yourself or someone else, and other topics that society still says women aren't supposed to be able to do well. Those girls grow into women who claim that they know nothing about money and can't even balance their bank account. They seem almost proud of it.

They let a husband, boyfriend, father or brother make their financial decisions, from which bills to pay to what investments to make. Then one day that someone else is not there, and the women are set adrift in a world of bills, finance charges, and retirement planning.

They don't know their financial planner, if there is one, and the planner doesn't know their needs, their goals, or their circumstances. Far too many find that they don't have enough money to live on. They have to work harder and longer than they expected. Some can't seem to get out of debt and be financially stable ever again.

Statistically, women tend to outlive men. They also tend to make less money than men over their careers, and to take career breaks for caregiving more than men do. As a result, they retire with smaller pensions and are at greater risk of poverty later in life. Don't let that happen to you. Take control of your finances, so that your money lasts as long as you need it to.

Getting into difficult financial circumstances can happen to even the highest-paid Singlish executive. Losing your job can mean a long time without work. You might have to take a lower-paying job just to keep some money coming in. Caring for aging parents or getting sick yourself can also disrupt your finances.

Being Singlish won't necessarily prevent the disaster. But simple Singlish financial savvy can help you plan for the unexpected, so that if it happens, you are in a better position to deal with it.

The author and activist Barbara Ehrenreich wrote "the other side of the principle that a man should earn enough to support a family has been that a woman doesn't need enough to even support herself." [16] That's an incredibly powerful statement about an archaic view of why men and women earn money. The old view implies that only men support families, and that all men earn enough to pay all the bills. It also assumes that paying the bills is the only reason women work. You know that's not true.

What happens to the woman who can't support herself if her marriage or partnership falls apart? She will have no savings, and no way of earning enough money for food, shelter, and the other basic necessities. Don't let yourself fall into this situation. It's your hard-earned money. Save and invest it wisely. Make your money work hard for you.

What does it take to be a financially savvy Singlish woman? Not much at all: basic math, goal setting, the willingness to learn, and a bit of self-control. Any woman, whether or not she intends to stay single, can and should look after her own money.

If you already have some money saved, congratulations! If not, start saving now; it's never too late. The earlier in life you start saving, the longer your money can work for you. Save steadily and invest wisely and your money will build up over time. Thanks to the magic of compound interest, the earlier you start, the more your money will pay you back. Even if you start later in life, every dollar you save is another step on the path to financial security. Every little bit helps.

Focusing on finances is not about being materialistic; it's about making sure that you have what you need. Government and business pensions are great to have, but too much reliance on them puts a woman at great risk. What if the company goes bankrupt, like Enron in 2001? Thousands of Enron employees lost their savings when the company went under. What if the government changes the retirement age, or the amount they pay to retirees? Inflation alone can make it harder to survive on basic government pensions; the cost-of-living increases don't really keep up with your actual costs. Looking after your own finances throughout your life makes you less dependent financially on these outside supports.

Here's a key point that too many women miss: savings trumps salary. David Bach, author of *Smart Women Finish Rich*, points out that it's not how much you make that makes you rich, it's how much you keep.[2] He's right. A woman with a six-figure salary who spends it all on shoes and clothes will be far worse off in the long run than a woman who makes less but invests whatever she can. Stories of women who worked for years in menial jobs and died as millionaires are all over the internet. Their secret is always the same: they saved a little bit from every paycheck, invested it carefully, and didn't buy more than they could afford. You can do that too.

First and foremost, Singlish women support themselves and actively look after their own finances. It helps to learn the basics when you are young, but that's not essential. Anyone can learn this stuff. It's basically adding, subtracting, planning, and sticking with the plan, then enjoying the benefits later. It's all up to you. When you decide to live Singlish, you accept that YOU and only you are responsible for your standard of living. You take control of saving, budgeting, investing, and debt reduction.

If you've never thought about building your own nest egg, it can be a little intimidating. There's all that pressure to suddenly have a massive savings account, or the other (more destructive) pressure to get what you want right now. Retail therapy feels so good on a bad day. How do you resist it?

Basic Budgeting

First, take a deep breath. The basics are actually quite easy.

Before you can actively manage your money, you must understand where it is coming from (the Ins) and where it is going (the Outs). You need to know how much you earn, how much you spend, and how much you can save.

The best way to do that is with a budget. Now, I can hear you saying "Ugh! Spread-sheets, tracking, accountants, finance, bills - this is not fun and exciting!" Think again! Many women get a lot of satisfaction, and a greater feeling of control over their lives, just by doing this simple step. And even if you don't like doing it, it is important. Trust me, it's not that complicated.

Try this: take a blank piece of paper and draw a line down the middle to make two columns. At the top of one column, write Income. Below it, list the amount of your monthly pay, plus any other money that comes in reliably. This means salary from a second job, alimony or child support if the payments arrive on time regularly, pensions or anything else that you can count on 100%.

Don't include what you expect in a bonus (more on that in a minute), or the payments from your ex-boyfriend who says he really will pay you back, as soon as he gets his feet under him. Yes, I've been there too. He never did pay me back. It was an expensive lesson, but one I needed to learn.

The other column of your budget worksheet is for Expenses. On this side, list your various expenses and their amounts (rent or mortgage, phone, cable, internet, cell phone, car payments, gas and insurance, etc.). List everything you do regularly, or feel you can't live without. If you are a coffee lover, include your daily lattes. Into yoga? Write in the cost of your classes. Going out with friends goes on this list too. Don't forget bills that come in once or twice a year, like insurance. Be honest about what you spend on your activities; refer to your bank account or credit card bill if you aren't sure. Remember to include any credit card, school, or other debt you have. The sample budgeting list at the end of this book will help you get started.

When you've finished, subtract the outgoing money from the incoming money. If it's a positive number, fantastic! You can cover your bills. The rest is the maximum you can pay yourself in savings each month. Save as much as you can every month, without fail. If you don't think you have the discipline to make the payment to yourself each month, set up an automatic payment to a separate savings or investment account via online banking. The idea is to do it every month without thinking twice.

If the result of your calculation is a negative number, you are headed for disaster, spending more than you earn. That's called negative cash flow, and it's the fast lane to bankruptcy, debt, and other bad things. Be happy that you figured that out now, before things get worse.

If your cash flow is negative, take control. Go back through your list of expenses and strike off the things you can live without. You can find free yoga classes online and make your coffee at home to save money.

Keep going until your cash flow is positive. If you can't get there without cutting essential expenses like rent, utilities and food, you have to make bigger changes. That might mean taking a second job, asking for a raise, finding a less expensive place to live or a roommate.

Your goal is to do more than stay financially afloat. You want long term security, and to stop living from paycheck to paycheck. You can do it. You are Singlish and strong.

Paying Bills and Saving Money

For most of us, our salary is the largest inflow in our budget, and our ability to earn that salary is our biggest asset. Deciding how that money flows out again is extremely important. Use it wisely.

Start with the bills. Each month, first pay your essential bills and pay yourself. Each month you have a mortgage or rent, car payment, electricity, phone, cell phone, clothes, and more -everything that survived the budgeting exercise you just finished. Pay those bills first.

Then pay yourself again, putting that savings into a separate savings account, that pays some interest. Leave that money alone until you reach your savings goal, or until you are ready to invest it. When your salary increases, pay down debt or increase the amount you save rather than adding new expenses.

How much do you pay yourself? Look back at your budget sheet and work from there. My grandfather's rule was at least 10% of each month's salary and every bonus. Can you do that? Can you save more? Save as much as you can. This is part of the principle of looking after yourself: you are planning for the future, whether saving to buy a home, take a vacation, or for retirement.

I didn't always manage to save 10% when I started working, and I save a lot more now. The point is to always put aside something for the future, or for an unexpected emergency. Yes, you might have less money for optional things. But unless you have a trust fund, you never know when you might need it.

In a few pages, we'll look at how financial goals can help make saving feel more like an accomplishment, and less like denying yourself something you want.

What about bonuses, tax refunds and even inheritances? Treat bonus money like a bonus: something wonderful that you can enjoy, but don't expect to happen regularly. Many people plan on getting a bonus every year, and they spend it before the money actually comes in. Bad idea - if your company has a tough year you might not get a bonus. If you have already spent the money, all you have now is another debt to pay. Try to think about the bonus like a lottery jackpot. It probably won't come in, but if it does, you know what you want to spend it on. Every time you get an unexpected payment, follow the same rule about savings: save as much as you can, and at minimum pay yourself the same percentage from the bonus as you would from your regular income. If you have expensive debt, like a credit card or school loans, paying down these balances is a good use of bonus money too.

When I first started working, my bonus went into savings, to get my "take this job and shove it" pile built up to a 6-month safety net. I if ever lost my job, I wanted enough cash in the bank, separate from my investments, to survive for 6 months. After that, I saved for the down payment on a house. When I owned a house, I put half into savings and used the other half for home improvements. The second time I moved to Europe, part of it went to buy new furniture, including a fabulous dining room set that I will use for the rest of my life.

Work hard to pay down your debts. Try to live debt-free, except for perhaps a mortgage or car loan. Credit cards are a great convenience, until they encourage you to buy more than you can afford. When you make your budget, commit to paying off new charges on the card in full every month, and to reducing any outstanding balances as soon as possible. Otherwise you are paying the credit card company for the right to owe them money.

As I write this, annual interest rates on credit card balances can be 20% or higher. That means that if you carry a balance for a year, for every $100 of that balance, you owe an extra $20. So if you don't pay it in full, your debt is not the $100 you spent for the shoes, it's as much as $120. Ouch!

If you have lots of credit card debt now, make eliminating it one of your first financial goals. Read your credit card agreements to see how much interest you are charged on each one. Pick the one with the highest interest rate to pay off first. Experienced financial advisors often recommend paying off your consumer debt within 3 years. Then don't let it build up again.

Paying off school loans can be a huge drain, especially in the US. Education is one way forward to a better-paying job, and I encourage you to make the most of yours. If, like most of us, you use loans to pay for it, take note: some education loans come with surprisingly high interest rates. Be aware of how much you borrow and how much you owe, and pay these off as soon as you can. Make paying it all off within 7 years of graduation another financial goal. I know that can be quite tough but do your best. After it's paid off, whatever you used to spend on loan payments can go to your next priority, whether that's paying off another loan or saving.

What about home mortgages? Not everyone wants to own a home, though in the US it's still a common expectation. Most of us don't have the cash to buy a home outright. Fortunately there are tax benefits to owing a mortgage in many countries. I think of the mortgage on my home as a "good debt," because it has a solid asset that I use every day, and that asset has a value of its own. As long as I can afford the payments, I don't mind having this kind of debt.

The key to financial stability is to always know what you can afford, and not to spend more than that. How nice the clothes are, how good you would look driving around in that car, or how big the house is compared to your friend's house doesn't matter.

If your debt is really overwhelming and you can't figure out how to get control of it, try talking with a reputable debt-assistance program. In some countries, there are government agencies that can help you with this, and their help is often free.

If you don't have access to one of those, work with a reputable financial advisor. Financial advisor Christine Turner starts her clients with a 10-20-70 rule. It's simple: 10% of each paycheck goes to savings (sounds familiar, right?). The next 20% is for paying down your debt, including student or car loans, credit card debt, consolidation loans…basically anything not associated with a mortgage. The other 70% is for your other living expenses, including the mortgage if you have one.

Using Christine's rule, divide your yearly income by 5 to get the amount you should put towards paying off debt each year. Then divide your total debt by that number to see how many years it will take you to pay off the debt. If it's more than three years (or seven for school loans), you'll want to find ways to increase your income, or decrease your living expenses, without reducing your savings. Keep saving and investing; you will want that money later in life, and it should be working for you now.

Jane: Getting Out of Debt

At 28 Jane, an editor, makes $50,000 each year. She rents her apartment and has the car her parents gave her for graduation. She has $70,000 in debt: $40,000 in school loans and $30,000 in credit card debt.

Jane calculates how long it will take her to be out of debt:

$50,000 ÷5 = $10,000. This is her 20% of income, that she can use to pay off debt each year. At this rate, it will take her 7 years to pay it all off.

Jane and her financial advisor figure out how to allocate her payments to pay off each individual loan as quickly as possible. The payment from each paid-off loan is then added to the existing payment on the next loan. She doesn't take on any more debt and reduces her expenses wherever she can. Two years into the plan, Jane finds a better-paying job. Her additional income goes to savings and increasing the debt payments. Jane is debt-free in 5 years.

The Singlish woman thinks about the financial impact of her choices. She plans her finances for her whole life, and makes conscious choices about what she does and doesn't want, now and in the future. She acknowledges trade-offs and is scrupulously honest with herself about what decisions she makes and why.

You can handle unexpected or unavoidable debts, like medical bills, the same way. If you are already in over your head, get help from a reputable agency or advisor, decide what you can pay each month and do it. Do it every month, no matter what. It's the only way out of the hole.

Investing

No matter what you might have heard, investing wisely is really not that hard. Before you start investing, learn from reputable sources. The major brokerage houses run useful, easy to understand free seminars. If you work with a financial advisor, make them explain each investment so that you understand it.

If anything is unclear, keep asking questions until it makes sense. It's tempting to let someone else make your financial decisions. After all, that's what good girls do, right? But you are not a good little girl, you are a Singlish woman. You are the one who should make your financial decisions, and you can.

Start with the basics. Here's my simple version, with absolutely no guarantees about any particular type of return for your money. I'm not an expert financial advisor. It's just how I keep it straight.

More reward (read: higher interest rate) comes with more risk (read: lower likelihood of success). What's a low-risk debt? The classic one is US treasury bonds. The US government isn't going anywhere, so the bonds are very safe. On the other hand, the US government knows that lots of people will want to buy these low-risk bonds, so they don't pay much interest. Interest on an investment is the amount the issuer has to pay you, so that you will give them some of your money. Investments with a higher risk of failure, like "Samantha's Bikini Store in Alaska," have to pay you more interest to get you to give them your money.

Each of us has our own risk tolerance; in general, it's higher when you're younger. Younger people have more time to make up for their investment mistakes. When you compare two investments, remember this: higher payout = higher risk = greater likelihood that you could lose your investment, and not get any payout.

Don't risk more in a single investment than you can afford to lose. One guideline I used when starting out was not having any more than 5% of my total savings in any one investment. That way, if it didn't work out (and some of my investments didn't), my finances weren't hit too hard.

Get good advice for anything you don't understand. Bad advice is everywhere. Good advice is harder to find. Talk to people with expertise, like a good financial advisor. Beware of success bias, though: just because someone has done well in the stock market before doesn't mean they always will. I like Nassim Nicholas Taleb's explanation in *Fooled by Randomness*. He shows how successful traders often just ride the wave when the whole market is going well. The success goes to their heads, and they start believing that they really are predicting the market. When it starts to turn down (as it always does) they can't believe that they could be wrong, and they lose lots of money. If you invest with them, that's your money lost. All because the trader forgot that strong markets don't last forever.

Stay skeptical. If the investment, or your return on it, sounds too good to be true, it probably is. Even if it comes from someone you trust. I invested a couple of times on the advice of uncles who were also brokers. Both investments offered higher returns than I could get from stocks or bonds. It worked for a while, but the odds were against me and I lost my investment both times. Now I won't even talk about money with them; it keeps the family get-togethers a lot more pleasant. That might be a good rule too: don't mix family and investment advice.

Don't believe anyone who emails you promising to deliver a million dollars if you help them move money out of their country by giving them your account information. It's always a scam.

Take advantage of free investment money. In the US, this is often available in a company 401K program. A 401K is a specific type of investment account that is designed to help you save for retirement, and gives you some tax advantages. Your employer can contribute to your 401K account too. The name 401K refers to the section of the IRS tax code that describes these accounts.

If you are lucky enough to have access to a 401K, put in the maximum you can afford to. If your company makes matching contributions, put in at least up to the maximum that the company will match. Their match is free money, so take it. The same applies to pensions, deferred compensation, or similar programs in any country. Even better, at least in the US, the part of your salary that you put into the 401K is tax-free until you take it out. This may be the only time that something which sounds too good to be true really isn't.

If your company doesn't have a 401K, talk to your bank or an investment advisor about an Individual Retirement Account, or IRA. Outside the US, investigate similar opportunities. Many countries have at least one or two choices.

Know your limitations. Some of you will intuitively "get" investing. Some won't. That's fine. Stick with what you understand, and don't get in over your head. If your neighbor invests in derivatives and you don't understand them (I don't really), resist the peer pressure and stay away. Know what you know, and more importantly, know what you don't know. Don't get burned because you are too embarrassed to say you don't understand an investment, or don't want to take the risk.

Once you have recognized what you don't know about investing, you can learn what you want to, then use that knowledge to make smarter decisions. Or just stay away from the areas that seem too confusing.

Although a financial advisor can be a huge help, you don't necessarily need one for buying and selling basic stocks. Most big brokerage businesses allow you to trade online by yourself, and there are reliable trading platforms that are now 100% online. Trading by yourself can cost less, but you miss out on the expert advice. You have to choose what makes the most sense for you, knowing that it can change over time.

Regardless of whether or not you use a broker or financial advisor, you should still have some basic principles when investing. One common sense rule I learned from my father, grandfather, and uncles is to know the company and understand and preferably like its products, before you buy its stock. You don't necessarily need first-hand experience with their products, but you should be able to easily understand what they do. That keeps me away from the very risky tech investments. I don't understand many of them and can't really evaluate the risks, so I don't invest in them.

Another rule I follow is to buy stock in reliable, well-known companies that pay dividends. Dividends are the company's way of giving shareholders some of the profits that they make. It's like getting paid to let them have your money, and it's a nice bonus. I reinvest the dividends, in that company or another, so the money keeps working for me.

How can you learn about a company? Explore their website. Look at their social media feeds. Remember that these are really just advertising, so also read what the investment houses say about them.

I like to read the company's most recent annual report. I focus on the chairman's letter, the company's description of their performance that year, the footnotes to the financial reports (you find all kinds of interesting facts here), and the auditor's statement. I don't do any fancy analysis of the financial reports; I apply logic. Do 70% of their sales come from economies going into decline? I don't want that stock; it's too risky for me.

Many investors have personal rules about what they will or will not invest in. Some people don't buy stock in defense contractors because they don't like to support wars. Others invest in sustainable energy rather than fossil fuels. Your rules will align with your own ethical and moral principles. Make them clear to anyone who you let manage your investments, and be firm. Singlish women know what they want from their investments. They make well-thought-out decisions and stick with them.

Learn at least a little about the various kinds of assets, including cash, fixed income (investments that pay a specific amount each time period), and equities (stocks). Learn the difference between growth and income, and make a conscious decision about how much you want to emphasize one or the other. Understand how that is affected by your own tolerance for risk, and how soon you will need the money.

Be very honest about this with yourself and your financial advisor, if you have one. Deciding how much money goes into which type of investment (also called "asset allocation") is one of the most important decisions you can mane as an investor. It has a far bigger impact on your investment success than whether you invest in Apple or Microsoft. You can learn more about this on reputable sites like Investopedia.

Setting Financial Goals

Everyone needs long term and short term financial goals. They give you something to work towards, and achievements to celebrate (remember, celebrating success is part of the fourth Singlish Principle). Knowing that you are working towards a goal makes denying yourself something right now easier to bear. The right goals improve your quality of life down the road. Your goal could be a vacation, a new home, a pile of "take this job and shove it" money so you can quit your job, or a financially secure retirement at 50.

I try to have at least two goals in place all the time. One of mine always about saving for the future, and the other can be anything from a great vacation to a new couch. Before veterinary school, I saved for a microscope. I've heard of goals that included finishing a college degree without loans, taking a dream holiday, moving out of a shared apartment, or reaching a 'magic number' in net worth. Start setting your own goals, celebrating when you reach one, and setting the next one.

Diane's Vacation Plan

As a sales representative for a clothing company, Diane encourages stores to buy her company's clothing and helps them develop sales strategies. This is as close as she could get to her dream of being a designer; she lacked the talent for design school. Recognizing this, Diane made the Singlish decision to find another way into her chosen industry, and she loves her job.

In college, Diane travelled with 2 friends on their breaks, using money they earned during the semester. They want to do it again now. Diane knows that she has the money for a really fancy trip, but it would cost most of her savings. Instead, she decides how much she

is willing to spend, then allocates it according to what is important to her. She'll fly economy, then stay in 4-star hotels, and take a special guided foodie tour.
Diane's saving habits made this trip possible. She saves 10% of each paycheck for retirement, and her second goal is always something fun or exciting. Her next goal is a down payment on a condominium.

There's a lot more to managing money and financial planning than this short chapter. I'm just giving you basic tools to get started. A financial advisor makes sense for many people. If you use one, get references and referrals, and talk to several before you pick one to work with. Once you start working with her, ask questions, challenge her advice if you don't agree with it, and be sure that you understand the positives and trade-offs of the choices you make. Like all Singlish women, you will be the one to make the decisions about your money.

Take The Long View

Dinner out every night in your twenties is great. Annual spa trips in your forties are great too. A good meal and a roof over your head every night for the rest of your life, even if you live until 100, is even better. Consider all of these scenarios in your financial planning, so you have a good balance of long term security and short term enjoyment.

There is no leprechaun waiting to give you a pot of gold. If you want it, you have to earn it. And even if it is hard, getting on top of your finances, understanding your costs and living within your means is important. It gives you power and freedom to live a fabulous, independent Singlish life.

Eva's Planning Pays Off

Eva, now 72, lived her whole life as a proud Singlish woman. She loved being a journalist, had loving relationships but never married, and has a circle of close friends. She always looked after her health, eating well and playing basketball.

Eva always saved money, even when times were hard. Once, right after she bought her house and started paying a mortgage, she was fired. Thanks to her savings, she could pay the mortgage during the 6 months it took to find a new job.

Eva retired 5 years ago. She is financially comfortable, able to eat out a few times a month with friends and travel a couple of times a year. Eva knows that she can afford this life for another 20 years.

She doesn't know it yet, but in about 5 years Eva will break her hip and one arm in an accident. The Long Term Care insurance she enrolled in 30 years ago will pay for the help she needs while she heals. While her activities afterwards will be curtailed, Eva will die peacefully at 83, at home, with money left in her will for her favorite niece.

Earning and managing your own money could be the most important Singlish skill of all. Supporting yourself financially gives you the freedom to choose: where to live, how to live, whether to make a change. You are truly independent. Managing your money isn't as complicated as you might think. If I can do it, you can too.

Lizzie: Wow, I took a lot of notes. We might have to come back to this topic again, too.

Elizabeth: Yes, I am sure that we will. It took me a long time and a lot of talks with my financial advisor to learn this much, and I am still learning. For now, tell me what you wrote down as most important.

Lizzie: Well, first I need to do a budget, so that I know what I really spend every month. Then I need to decide what I want to do with my money: do I want to buy a car, or own a house, or travel? How long do I want to work? Things like that.

Elizabeth: Right, it's important to set goals. What else?

Lizzie: I need to get some advice and make sure I understand it. Then I decide how much to spend and save, and what to save for. I'm sure there will be trade-offs; I might have to cut back on buying new clothes all the time. But if it gets me closer to a goal that I really want, that's OK. I want to try that budget plan you talked about. It sounds easy.

Elizabeth: You are doing great. Besides knowing what you want and learning what you need to be able to make and stick with your decisions, did you learn anything else?

Lizzie: Yes, I have to be honest with myself, even if it hurts. If I cheat on my plan, I need to figure how to avoid doing it again, and move on. If I really don't understand something I need to speak up and say so, not just pretend that I know the answer. My decisions are too important to fake it.

Elizabeth: That's a really good start. You can definitely handle this.

Lizzie: I guess my start will actually be pretty small. First jobs don't pay a lot in my field. But if I understood correctly, every little bit helps, and the earlier I start making my money work for me, the more it will pay off. Right?

Elizabeth: Right.

Applying Singlish Principles to Personal Finance

- Know what you want, and manage your money to help you get it.
- Think about your financial and savings decisions and stand by them.
- Be honest with yourself about your needs, wants, income and debt. Know the difference between what you want and what you need.

- Look after yourself by planning for the short and long term. Prince Charming and your fairy godmother will not take charge of your finances. Build the fabulous life you want for yourself.
- Celebrate each time you reach a financial goal. Then set the next one and go after it.

Your Own Home

Lizzie: That was a lot of information about money! I think I understand and can take it one step at a time. Now I have another question. When you told me about saving you said, 'my house.' Do you really own your own house? I would love to own a house! How did you buy it? What is it like to own a house?

Elizabeth: Don't look so surprised! If you follow the financial planning steps and stick with the principles, you can do this. Which ones do you think apply?

Lizzie: Well, know what you want and tell yourself the truth have to be part of it. And I guess stand by your decisions and

financial goals, because a goal this big can take a long time to reach.
Elizabeth: Right! And celebrate your successes along the way. Here's how I did it....

One of the most exhilarating moments of a Singlish life is the first time you move into your own home. It doesn't really matter whether it is an apartment or a house, or if you lease it or buy it. What matters is that you live there, and not with your parents. If you share it with a friend or roommate, that still counts. Your roommate is an equal, and you make the decisions about it together, as equals.

In the twenty-first century, we expect women to live alone or with someone who is not a parent or partner at some point in their lives. But that was not always the case.

In early twentieth century America, when single women began entering the workforce as "shop girls" (store clerks), secretaries, or in similar roles, they faced two major problems if they didn't want to live at home. First, they weren't paid much, so affording a place of their own was a financial challenge. Second, there weren't many places that would sell or rent to single young women.

Society's assumption was that these women were somehow deficient in morals or money. A single woman would not be able to afford a place of her own, so she was a bad risk. If she could afford it, many people thought that the only way she could earn enough money was through prostitution. Either way, no one wanted her. Take a moment to be glad you are alive in the twenty-first century…. I certainly am!

Sometimes solutions did appear. New York City, with its large population of single women coming from all over the country, had a few places just for women. In 1905, ship owner John Arbuckle docked the *Jacob A. Stamler* at a pier and rented rooms to single girls who would "behave with honor." [24] It was a revolutionary idea for its time. Unfortunately, it only lasted until August 1915.

The Barbizon Hotel and the Trowmart Inn provided other alternatives later in the century.

The Trowmart Inn opened in New York City in 1910. [43] To live there, a single woman had to be younger than 35, working but without enough money to live anywhere she chose, and "of good quality," as documented by references. Women rented single or double rooms, all of which had shared baths, as was common for the time. The hotel also had a library, laundry, a dining room, and rooms for needlework and social events, as well as a "female physician" on site. Located near public transportation, shops and factories, it sounds like it was a good place to live for the time.

More famous, even into the middle of the twentieth century, was the Barbizon Hotel, also in

New York City. The Barbizon opened in 1927 and was also for "quality" girls, with references required. Applicants were also rated for looks, dress, and overall demeanor. The Barbizon had a reputation as the place where the most beautiful single women coming to New York City lived. The hotel also had in-house supervision and became known as a place where girls could hold onto their virginity, although as Michael Callahan reported in Vanity Fair in 2010,[6] some women learned how to get around the rules.

Some very famous women lived there before they became famous, like Joan Crawford and Grace Kelly. Less well-known are the women who never left. Known as "the Women," some became successful career women and were the Singlish women of their time.

Fortunately, in our time, things are much easier. You can live alone, and if you want to, you can own your own home.

What Can You Afford?

Knowing what you can afford is the first step towards having your own place. Absolute honesty with yourself, the Singlish way, is absolutely required. This is no place to hide from your financial truth.

If you haven't already done so, complete the budget exercise we looked at earlier, using the template in Appendix 1 to help you. Figure out what you can afford to pay every month, just in rent or mortgage. Then consider the other expenses, searching out costs in your area. These include heating, water, garbage removal, cable, phone, power, internet access, parking, and food. Don't forget the costs that aren't monthly: renters or homeowner's insurance, security deposits or down payments. What about set-up costs, like furniture, dishes, pots and pans, towels, sheets?

Compare those costs with the cost of apartments or homes in the place you wish to live. Work from the salary you have now, not the raise you hope to get in 6 months. If you can't afford to move there right now, set a financial goal to help you get there, or look for more affordable alternatives. Assume that you will need to pay 20% of the total cost of the home as your down payment. This gives you instant equity, and also prevents you from having to buy mortgage insurance, which would add another cost.

Because we often think of a mortgage as good debt, some people don't realize what it really is. A mortgage is a loan, with the house as your security. When you have a mortgage, the bank has the right to take away your home if you can't make the payments every month.

Keep the mortgage to the minimum you need, and the monthly payments at a level you can easily afford. If you get into financial trouble and can't make the payments, you can lose your home. The same goes for the size of your rental payment. If you can't afford the rent, you can be evicted. Don't let that happen to you. Think smart, think Singlish.

Once you have worked out your budget, decided whether you want to rent or buy and how much you can spend, and you have the money you need, it's time to think about a mortgage. Don't apply for a bigger mortgage than you can comfortably afford to pay off, even if the bank offers it. Decide what you want to spend and then stick with that decision. You'll be happy that you did.

In the US, it's best to pre-apply for a mortgage. Work with a banker to complete the paperwork, and get confirmation of the loan approval in writing. Your purchase will be much smoother. If you end up bidding against someone for a property and they don't have the pre-approval, the fact that you do could tip the balance in your favor.

Shop Smart

Always make a shopping list before you start to look at properties. Make a list of "must-haves" and "nice to haves" for your new home. Does it have to be a detached home, or would you consider a townhouse with neighbors on either side? Is a second or third bedroom optional or essential? Do you care if the kitchen appliances are gas or electric? Is off-street parking important? If you're in a multi-story building, do you want one with a lift? Is ground floor living acceptable, or do you want to be higher up? Whatever is important to you, figure it out and write it down, so you can consider how well the potential homes you view will meet your needs. There's an example in Appendix 2 to get you started.

Once you have the budget and your wish list worked out, it's time to go looking for your home. It's fun and exciting, so enjoy it!

Depending on where you live, you may be able to view properties alone, or you may need to work with a rental or sales agent. Agents usually work via contracts; read the contract carefully before signing it. Make sure you understand any fees and what you are paying for.

Bring a friend along to the viewings if you can. A friend is not as emotionally caught up in the decision. She can point out things that you, in your euphoria, might overlook. Besides, it's more fun when there are two of you!

If you are working with an agent, share your "must have" and "nice to have" lists with him or her, and insist that they stick to it. If they show you a flat that's missing something on your "must have" list, point that out. This is no time to be overly sensitive to hurting someone's feelings. You are shopping for your home. Stand up confidently and state what you want, like the strong Singlish woman you are.

If the agent keeps showing you places that don't match your instructions, ask them why. Make sure that your requests are reasonable. Check online for places that match your list. Don't assume that the agent knows what's best for you. If you believe that the properties you are looking for do exist, and the agent is just not showing them to you, change agents. Do it politely, but do it.

Fast forward again now: you have found your new home. There are a few things to do or look for before you close the deal and move in.

If you are renting, read the rental contract and have a lawyer look at it for you. Make sure you understand and can agree with everything before you sign. Ask questions, get any troublesome clauses changed. You'll pay the lawyer, but it is money well spent.

Find out where the garbage and recycling are thrown out, when they are picked up, how to reach the landlord and whether there is a superintendent on site. Also check how much notice you have to give for departure, and how often the rent can be changed. Find out what the normal rent increase is.

Ask about the neighbors, and try to meet one or two if you can. Find out about building or neighborhood rules or norms. In my building, we expect to be able to sleep between 10 PM and 7 AM, though we are not super-strict. In my previous building, everyone was very strict about not doing laundry on the weekends, and I had to adjust while

I lived there. Learn what you can before you make up your mind. If you don't think you can be comfortable there, don't sign the lease.

If you are buying a home, the list is a little different. Pay for a professional title search, so you are sure that no one else has a claim to your house. Your lawyer will often take care of that. Hire a home inspector, then read the report. It will tell you whether you can expect to need to do any major repairs soon, like fixing the roof, or dealing with problems with the heating or water system. You might be able to have the seller fix it and prove the repairs with documentation, or negotiate the price down if you will have to pay for the repair work. A good real estate agent can advise you.

If you can't come to agreement, walk away. There will be other houses that are just as good for you, or better. When I looked for my first house, I found one that I really liked. However, I smelled gas in one part of the ground floor. The home inspector smelled it to, and couldn't find a source, so I did not buy the house. It just wasn't worth the risk.

Just as you would if you were renting, try to meet the neighbors, and find out about the building or neighborhood norms. Most importantly, make sure your lawyer reviews the sales contract, and that you understand it completely. Don't sign any paperwork for the purchase until you are satisfied.

<u>Melanie: Finding Her First Home</u>

Melanie, 26, will graduate this year and move to another city for her first job. She needs a place to live. After paying her school and car loans and other critical expenses, her budget allows $1000/month for rent and other housing costs like utilities and insurance. Melanie would like to live alone, but an online search makes it clear that she can't afford it. She starts looking for a roommate, asking friends and family for ideas. One friend's sister is also looking for a home in that town. The two women decide to move in together. They combine their "must-have" and wish lists, go on some viewings, and find a place that meets their needs. They both sign the contract as equals.

Melanie's total home costs are now $750/month. Each month she saves the extra $250 towards a down payment on her own place. She also sets a goal of performing well enough at work to earn a promotion and raise in two years. By working smart as well as hard, documenting her successes, and asking for what she wants, Melanie gets that promotion. She saves enough money to buy her first home before she turns 30.

Living on your own, and even owning your own home if that's what you want, is within reach for every Singlish woman. There's something special about a place that matches your style, where you feel completely comfortable. Do you want your own home? What steps will you take to make that wish come true?

Lizzie: I would love to have my own place! I like to decorate, and I can fill it with furniture and souvenirs from trips, and have parties with my friends.
Elizabeth: Well, you can do it. Have you thought about what you really want in a home, and what you can afford?
Lizzie: Not really, no. I guess my first step is to make that list of "must haves" and "nice to haves." Then I can think about a budget, based on what I think I can earn when I start working. With that information, I can set a goal, and make a plan for buying my own home.
Elizabeth: Perfect. You understand exactly what I have been saying. I know you can do this!

Applying Singlish Principles to Having Your Own Home

- Know what you want for your home. Don't compromise to make an agent happy. Get the facts, understand what's realistic, and then decide.
- Stand by your decisions. Decide on a limit to how much you can spend on your home, or that you will save monthly to get it, then stick with it. It's worth it.

- Have fun looking for your next home, share the search with a friend if you can, and celebrate when you find it.
- Be truthful about what you can afford. Make sure you can manage the payments comfortably.

Living The Fabulous Life: Fun and the Singlish Woman

"Even though you are growing up, you should never stop having fun."

Nina Dobrev, Actress

Lizzie: That was a pretty intense discussion. Work, money, owning a home…they are all so serious. They are important, no question, but can we talk about something fun for a little while?

Elizabeth: Sure, that was a lot to digest. We can always talk more about it another time. For now, should we talk about having fun without having a boyfriend?

Lizzie: Yes! Everyone my age seems to be pairing up, and since I don't want to, I feel weird going out with couples all the time. How do I have just as much fun without a boyfriend?

Elizabeth: You have fun the same way you always have: doing things that you like with people you like. You can also learn to do things alone. Movies, meals, museums, concerts…even vacations.

Lizzie: Vacations? No way! I can't imagine going away by myself! I just figured that I would have to wait until I had a boyfriend, or maybe another single friend.

Elizabeth: Why wait? Going with another single friend is a good start, but you can also go alone. The principles here are to try new things and have fun. Then celebrate your successes. The best vacation I ever took alone was….

There's no reason to let life pass you by when you are Singlish! Great experiences are happening every day, and the Singlish woman wants to be part of them. She puts herself out in the world and lives her life to the fullest.

Going it Alone

Some people wonder how the Singlish woman has fun when her friends aren't available. It's really not that hard. Figure out what you like to do. Then do it, all by yourself. If you're nervous, start with something easy like going to a movie. You can get there just before the show starts, and once the lights go out no one is looking at you anyway. At the end, you have seen the movie and can talk about it with your friends or at work. No one has to know that you went alone unless you choose to tell them.

Watching people is also great fun. I started in the coffee houses in Europe, where they let you nurse a cup of tea or glass of wine for hours. I bring a book to read (or pretend to read) and watch people to my heart's content. Las Vegas casinos are really good for this too. Get yourself a drink and watch the show. People really believe no one in Las Vegas is looking at them!

Look for similar opportunities where you live. Starbucks and other coffee shops, where people gather to talk, work, or just take a break from the world, were designed for you to drop in any time. Spend enough time there and you can meet the other regulars and even make new friends. Many European countries are full of places like this; Vienna and Paris had famous cafe cultures long before Starbucks existed. Cafes are easy places to go to alone; no one looks at you as if you were odd.

I like going to public libraries with comfortable reading chairs. I can relax, read, or watch people, and books are an easy way to strike up a conversation if I want to talk with someone.

Once you are comfortable doing a few things alone, branch out. Try going to a museum, art show or concert by yourself. Take a walk, visit a local historical site, or go sightseeing in your hometown. Nothing about these activities actually requires anyone else to enjoy. Don't deny yourself their pleasure just because you're on your own.

Sharon Goes to a Concert

Sharon, is a huge Johnny and the Gemtones fan, and she had always wanted to see them in concert. None of her friends ever wanted to go with her, so she never went to a show. When the band announced a farewell tour, she realized that she had to go, even if it meant going alone. She bought a single ticket – and because it was a single, she got a great seat. At the concert, the people next to her thought she had come with someone who bought a single seat somewhere else. She didn't see any reason to correct them; it was just a way to start a conversation. Once the music started, nothing else mattered anyway. Sharon had a great time, dancing and singing along with all of her favorite songs. It was a fabulous night!

Finding Friends

If you are not comfortable going out by yourself, do what Valerie did in the Romance chapter. She could have met a new friend at the planting day as easily as a new boyfriend. Join a community event that interests you and meet your neighbors. Take a class at the local community center. Try a cooking class; there is something about food that is inherently social. One of my friends is an avid bicyclist; during a temporary assignment in a new town, she joined a cycling group and had an instant social life outside of work.

Try something new or something familiar. Choose from the opportunities available in your town. If you meet someone in one of these classes with whom you like talking, invite them for a coffee afterwards. Pick an activity you like or want to learn, be yourself, be open to talking to new people, and see what happens.

Inviting Friends to Join You

Too often, we assume that couples will only want to be with other couples. But a Singlish woman's circle of friends is broad enough to include friends who don't think that way, or couples who don't feel they have to do everything together all the time.

Don't assume that your friends won't want to join you; invite them along! Whether it's a play, concert, trip to the zoo, hike, lecture…anything at all. The Singlish woman is confident and happy to include her friends in her activities. She doesn't think she has to wait for them to include her in theirs.

Travel

Traveling has traditionally been one of the challenges for single women. But a Singlish woman does not let these outdated traditions stop her. She just plans for any challenges that might arise. Thousands of women travel to new places by themselves, and you can too. I have explored England, Czech Republic, Austria, Scotland, Slovenia, Croatia, France, Germany, Hungary, Italy, and the rest of Switzerland, plus Australia, Canada, and parts of Brazil, Thailand and India – and I did most of it alone. How? Well, I travelled smart. Here are some tips that might help you. They apply to any trip, whether it is to another country, or another town just up the road.

Have a plan, or at least a skeleton of a plan, for your trip. Know the broad outlines of what you want to see, so that you don't spend your time wandering around aimlessly and missing "the good stuff." Check out Atlas Obscura, TripAdvisor, other travel sites and the local website for your destination. Download some podcasts to learn more about the history, food, or culture of your destination. Sometimes you can find podcasts with walking tours; I like the Bowery Boys Podcast for New York City.

Do some research before your trip. Which areas are safe or best avoided? Where can you stay? Is public transportation reliable? If you are exploring a new culture, investigate the local customs regarding women alone, bargaining in shops, and other behaviors you find normal. Look online, or ask friends and colleagues about their experiences.

Learn a few words in the local language. Even just the basics like please, thank you, excuse me, and "where is the toilet?" will go a long way. And it never hurts to be able to say "I'm sorry, I only speak (you fill it in here)" in the local language. It's just good manners.

Don't take unnecessary risks. If your research says that women walking alone at night will be considered prostitutes, pay attention. You can still go to the hot new restaurant and enjoy the meal. Just take a taxi or Uber back to the hotel after dinner.

Speaking of hotels and restaurants, stay at reputable hotels. Check the online reviews, and consider trying a local chain. Or look for an Airbnb in an interesting location, and find out what local life is like. Visit the shops, find a local cafe, and feel the vibe. Stretch yourself.

Use your contacts. If you know someone from the area, ask them to recommend a hotel, restaurants, or something to see that most tourists miss. There's nothing like advice from a native to improve your experience. If you belong to an organization like the Rotarians, or your college alumni society, use them to seek out contacts. If you know someone in the armed services stationed in that country, contact them. Most expats love to hear from visitors from home, and they are usually generous with their advice. Bring them a little something from home (a favorite food is often welcome) to say thank you.

If you want to see the main sights in a big city easily and you have limited time, try a bus tour. Although they can be kind of corny, the "step on/step off" buses show you the highlights, with explanations in your own language. They are also warm and dry in bad weather.

You may be thinking that these are good tips for any traveler, male or female, single or not. If so, you get the point: being Singlish means experiencing all the adventure in life that our coupled counterparts do. It's just a matter of using one's head. Don't restrict yourself to visiting well known areas. Plan trips through the lesser-known Greek Islands, or through Eastern Europe, South America, or anywhere else you want to go. Do it wisely, but do it.

Marianne's Dream Holiday

Marianne, 32, works in a major Parisian department. She has always dreamed of a safari vacation but was afraid to go by herself. Then one day she saw an advertisement in the paper for a guided tour of Namibia with a small group. Drinking her coffee and staring at the pictures, Marianne decided that it was time for her to finally make that dream come true. The company *would arrange everything. Their customers were usually about her age, although they were more often couples than singles. Marianne almost changed her mind about going when she saw that, but then decided that she wasn't going to let it stop her.*

She arranged her vacation from work and took a 10-day safari trip across Namibia. The scenery and the animals were even more impressive than she imagined. There was an awkward moment when one of the other women asked how she lost her husband, but Marianne just laughed and explained that she was traveling alone and did not want to miss this experience. No one else ever mentioned it. Marianne came home with hundreds of photos and amazing memories. She's already planning her next trip.

If you're still not sure about traveling alone, especially to someplace exotic like Marianne did, look online for companies specializing in small group trips, or trips for small groups of women. Use them for your window into an adventure trip, or just to see someplace new and meet new people. I'm saving for a horseback riding trip in Iceland. It combines my favorite activity of riding with a place I would love to see, and guarantees that I will have people to say 'wow' with.

Social Entertaining

Inviting people to your home is one of the best ways to build friendships. Invitations signal to acquaintances that you would like to know them better, and strengthen ties with people you already know well. And the definition of "entertaining" is very flexible! It can be a formal sit-down dinner, a fancy dress or costume party, barbeque in the back yard or just drinks and snacks. You also get to choose how many people to invite, and which ones. Bringing people into your home is a great way to build friendships, so give it a try. Yes, the old phrases like "three's a crowd," and "I'd be a third wheel" can make it feel a little weird to invite couples to your home when you are single. Ignore that. Why shouldn't you invite friends over? Relax, be confident and comfortable in your Singlish life, and have some fun.

Look for entertainment that is easy to manage alone. If you keep the food light and don't make a sit-down dinner, clean-up is easy to do alone too. Here are some ideas for easy Singlish entertaining:

• Center your invitation around an activity: a particularly good movie, political debate on TV, or sporting event that you want to watch.

• Tie your party to a holiday: St. Patrick's Day, Christmas, or your country's national holiday are always good inspirations.

• Make a small get-together with just a few good friends that you haven't seen in a while, serve coffee and cake or wine and snacks, and settle in for some catching up.

Entertaining friends also lets you experiment. I love to cook but don't always want to follow a recipe. I like to have at least one new dish on the table each time I host a dinner. My friends know that meals at my house are normally tasty but may be a bit of an adventure. I lean towards simple recipes, easy to prepare but with a good flavor, so that I can enjoy my company and not be stuck in the kitchen. There are a few examples in Appendix 3, to show you what I mean and to inspire your own cooking.

Over the course of a year, I'll host cocktail parties, sit-down dinners, coffee and cake sessions, or just informal drinks with munchies. It's all very relaxed; that's the beauty of entertaining your friends. If the glassware doesn't all line up neatly on your table, they will forgive you. You can all relax and have fun.

Your Singlish self is interesting, fun, and doesn't let being alone keep her from enjoying life. Get your friends together and make some memories.

Business Entertaining

Business entertaining is different than getting together with friends. Many jobs require business dinners, including hosting clients or vendors, or that odd fusion of business and social time when you entertain colleagues. Dining with colleagues and their spouses or partners builds relationships that can help you throughout your career and make your work days more enjoyable. Find a way to make non-work connections with married co-workers or, as Eric Klinenberg[28] points out, you may be cut out of networks important for career progress. Invest in these connections early in your career and they can pay off later.

My parents invited clients or business partners to our house for dinner all the time. As I grew older, I would help my Mom in the kitchen, freeing her to spend more time with the guests. So I knew how complicated it could be. I also saw the benefits. Many deals were struck and problems solved as they all sat around the table. For a small businessman like my dad, that was absolutely essential.

Early in my corporate career I used to do sit down dinners for colleagues at home, complete with fancy table settings and 4 course menus. I quickly realized that to make that work, I needed to clone myself. So I limited my home entertaining to personal friends, and kept the business meals outside. We're all different; if you can manage the food, décor, cleaning up, and general hosting duties while still spending time with your guests, go for it.

I find that business entertaining in public spaces is easier. It's certainly less intimate, and that helps you avoid awkward misunderstandings if you are having dinner with a man. Plus, someone else does the work for you, and everyone can eat what they want. Be aware that the staff's tendency is still to give the bill to a man. If you are the hostess, be sure to arrange for the check to be given directly to you well in advance. Remember, this is business entertaining, not a date, and not time to be demure.

Another solution to the problem of entertaining colleagues is to throw one large event each year. For several years, I threw a holiday season cocktail party. I invited everyone I knew and their spouses. Hot and cold finger foods and a full bar, some back-ground music, candles and non-denominational seasonal decor, and I solved my obligations for the year. Then I slept for 2 days to recover! Summer or autumn barbeques can be good ways to do this too, and if the weather is good you will have less mess in the house to clean up.

Maria and the Management Team Dinner

Maria, 30, is the highest performing sales representative in her region. She sells large construction equipment, like earthmovers and dump trucks, to companies that build skyscrapers across the country. Last month, the Vice President of Sales visited Maria's best client, BBDG Construction, with her. Maria hosted a dinner for her Vice President, BBDG's President and herself, as part of the visit. She wanted BBDG to order two new pieces of equipment and needed the dinner to go smoothly.

Because it was not in her hometown, she called the hotel concierge in advance for restaurant recommendations. When making the reservation, Maria explained the nature of the dinner, and that she would pay the bill. When they arrived for dinner she spoke briefly to the maître d' and reminded him of their discussion.

All went smoothly until the bill arrived. The waiter tried to give it to the President of BBDG. Maria calmly put out her hand for the bill and said "I'll take care of the paperwork, thank you." The waiter looked surprised but gave it to her, and she paid without further incident.

Walking out of the restaurant, Maria's Vice President complemented her on the dinner and her handling of the account. Best of all, BBDG ordered their new equipment the next day!

Whether you entertain formally or informally, at home or out at a restaurant depends on your own preferences. Try a few different ideas to find the ones that you like best, then stick with them, at least for business. After just a few tries you will be a Singlish hostess with her own special style and confidence.

Elizabeth: So you see, there are lots of ways to have fun by yourself, just like there are lots of ways to have fun with friends. You just need to be a little bit brave.

Lizzie: Yes, I see. Now is as good a time as any for me to try new things. If I can find other people with the same interests, I might even make some new friends.

Elizabeth: That's right. People want to be friendly with other people who have fun doing the things they enjoy. Where will you start?

Lizzie: I'm still a little nervous about this, you know. I'm not sure that I am up to throwing a big party alone, or going out to dinner by myself. I think I'll start with a movie. There's a new one that I want to see that my friends aren't interested in. I was going to wait for it to come out online, but I'll go see it in the theater myself. It would be a good study break.

Elizabeth: Good choice! You can tell me about it at our next lunch. You know, it's important to learn to do things by yourself. We're all likely to be alone at some point in our lives, so this is like practicing for the future.

Lizzie: I know — that's another one of the principles!

Applying Singlish Principles to Fun and Entertainment

- Have fun! Go places, see the sights, and enjoy yourself. Consider each new experience a success you can celebrate.

- Try new things. You don't need anyone's permission to learn a new hobby, host your first party, or travel to a new place. Make your plans and do it.

Living Well

Elizabeth: Let's talk about what living well really means. What does it mean to you?

Lizzie: Well, living well means being healthy, and earning enough money to do interesting things and not worry about where my next meal will come from.

Elizabeth: Good, what else does it mean?

Lizzie: I guess it means enjoying life, too. Not just getting up every day and taking a walk, but enjoying a walk around town, stopping in to look at the shops, maybe meeting a friend for coffee, and having those friends and fun experiences we talked about.

Elizabeth: Do you think you will live well?

Lizzie: I think I live well now. Because you're asking, I guess there is something a Singlish woman has to prepare for, if she wants to live well her whole life. Am I right?
Elizabeth: Yes, you are! Living well for a long time means planning and looking after your-self now. You have to tell yourself the truth about what you're capable of, and as you get older there will be some limitations you have to adjust for. Most of all, you need to keep your sense of humor and have fun.
Lizzie: What does living well mean to you?
Elizabeth: For me, living well means….

Living well has many meanings. What do you picture when you think about living well? I think of being outdoors, eating delicious food, maybe spending time with horses, getting enough sleep, and generally having something to smile about every day.

Too many people think living well is all about diet and exercise. Did you know that the origin of the dreaded word "diet" is the Greek word, diaeta? Neither did I. The really interesting part is that to the Greeks, diaeta was about more than food. It described an entire way of life, including mental and physical ways to health, not just a way to lose weight. I love this concept because it includes many of the ideas that go into living well. Health is about more than weight, and the way you live your whole life, your diaeta, is more than just what you do or do not eat.

Singlish women want to live well, to have interesting and fun experiences, and make the most of the time they have. In this chapter we'll look at how the Singlish woman looks after herself, so that she can live well.

What can you do for your diaeta? Eat right, sleep well, get some exercise, have friends, stay involved with people and activities you enjoy. Doing any one of these is not hard; doing them all, and making time for them in a busy life, can take some effort. But if I can do it, you can too. Here's what I have learned:

Eating Well

There are thousands of sites and books telling you the "secret" to eating. Superfoods, supplements, detoxes: you name it, there are books telling you how it is the only secret to a perfect diet. I say that moderate eating is the best way to go. It's what our bodies evolved to handle, not All You Can Eat buffets and Super Size servings of fries. Eating well, and changing from a few big meals to delicious smaller meals with healthy snacks in between, has given me much more energy and stamina.

So much of what we eat is mental. We eat under stress, eat to get rid of boredom, eat as part of socializing. We eat foods that are trendy to look cool. We even go on diets to be part of the crowd.

Or we torture ourselves with comparisons of how much or what we eat versus what our friends or co-workers eat. Enough already! Your body and brain need energy. Food is how you get it. Tasty, satisfying, healthy food can also be easy and fun, and you don't have to beat yourself up about what you do or don't eat. Stop calling yourself a dieter.

Let's look at what I consider the real basics for good eating that a Singlish woman should know. I learned much of this from Patti Milligan, Partner and Director of Performance Nutrition at TIGNUM, a company that helps executives maintain high levels of performance despite tight schedules, travel, and high-stress environments.[37] These tips help me stay healthier at home and on the road. They can help you too.

Eat brightly colored foods. That means lots of fresh vegetables and fruits. These are "free" for me; whenever I want fresh vegetables, I eat them. My meals have a lot of vegetables too, and then I fill them out with a bit of protein and starch. Stay away from pre-made foods, fried things, and very salty or fatty foods.

One of Patti's tips was to pick at least 3 different colors from the salad bar, besides the dressing. It's an easy rule to follow, and one that holds when making salads at home too. Think about the color of those fried and fatty foods – many of them are white or dull brown.

Don't deny yourself a food absolutely. In my experience, this only makes the cravings worse. Then you eat everything is sight to make up for the denial. It just doesn't work. Figure out how small a portion will satisfy your craving, eat that much, then move on without guilt. I'm still a chocoholic, but I know that one square of 70% chocolate is just as satisfying as a whole milk chocolate bar. So I go for the 70% square and don't agonize over it. Maybe one cookie is enough to stop your craving; if so, eat it, enjoy it, and go back to your regular life.

Change your snacks. Sure, we all love a good snack. I can't get through a day without some chocolate. Snacking throughout the day can be very healthy, if you do it right. A smart snack helps to keep your energy up, keep your brain engaged and working at its best. It's actually better for your body to eat several small meals throughout the day, rather than 3 big ones.

The secret is to pick the right snacks. Candy bars, cakes and cookies are delicious, but they get you right back onto the sugar roller coaster. You eat the candy, your blood sugar goes up, you feel lots of energy. Then soon after, your blood sugar crashes and you are hungry, tired and cranky all over again. You look for another snack and start the cycle again.

Instead, try something just as tasty but a bit better for you. There are plenty of sweet fruits and vegetables. Apples are easy to carry and have plenty of water and fiber. Apple slices with a little bit of nut butter also have some protein. Vegetables like carrot sticks, sweet peppers and sugar snap peas are tasty and have a satisfying crunch that is even better than fried potato crisps. Healthy nut snacks (with lots of nuts and berries, not a lot of chocolate bits) give you a mix of energy, vitamins, and protein.

Keep your portion sizes reasonable. A handful of nuts, one apple, or one sweet pepper cut up will be sufficient. Here are some ideas for better snacking:

• Small handful of roasted, unsalted almonds, walnuts, sunflower seeds or pumpkin seeds

• One raw apple

• Sliced vegetables (carrots, sweet peppers, snow peas, celery, asparagus, jicama)

• One hardboiled egg

At every opportunity: water, water, water! Add some lemon or ginger to make it taste better. Or drink caffeine-free tea.

Look at how, when, and why you snack. Do you eat because you are bored? Stressed? Lonely? Do you have to eat something at the same time every day? Or every time you sit down with a colleague over coffee? Once you understand your snacking pattern, you can make it into something that helps you stay energized. If you always get hungry at mid-afternoon and can't resist a trip to the chocolate stash, try eating some fruit or nuts about 30 minutes before your normal snack time. If you walk to the snack bar and buy something without being hungry, try taking a brief walk in another direction instead. Maybe you're actually thirsty, not hungry. Try a non-caffeinated drink before reaching for the snack. Find out what your body really needs.

Read labels! Since I am a celiac (someone who must avoid gluten for medical reasons), I have been a label reader for many years. Food labels have so much information, but so few people read them. It's actually not that hard to find and read the ingredient section.

One easy rule to improve food choices is to only buy foods with ingredients that you recognize and can picture. That takes out most of the highly processed foods. I mean, what is sodium diacetate and what is it doing in my food anyway?

Look closely at anything that is a low fat or fat free version of an original food. Fat gives food texture, and helps it stick to your taste buds. Take it out, and you need to find other ways to make the food taste good. Companies will often add more sugar or artificial sweeteners than are in the original to improve the flavor of the fat-free version.

What about those healthy snack bars that seem to be everywhere these days? Well, here's some more info I learned from Patti: you have to read these labels too! They are not always as healthy as you might think. Bars that claim to give you energy

Values Per Bar	Yumjunque Candy Bar	Masquerading Bar	Better Bar
Calories	220	200	210
Calories From Fat	120	50	90
Total Fat	13 grams	5 grams	6 grams
Saturated Fat	8 grams	2 grams	1 grams
Total Carbohydrates	30 grams	35 grams	30 grams
Fiber	1 gram	3 grams	6 grams
Sugars	26 grams	25 grams	15 grams
Protein	2 grams	4 grams	12 grams
Sodium	150 mg	260 mg	20 mg

often do it with sugar or caffeine. Compare the labels of some "healthy" snack bars to candy bar labels and you might be surprised.

Let's compare three imaginary product labels. They are all based on actual products available today:

Surprised? That Masquerading Bar may look healthy (low fat) but look closer: it's almost as high in sugar as the candy bar, has very little protein ….and look at all that sodium! Not so healthy after all, is it?

I look for bars with at least 10g protein, carbohydrates that don't all come from sugar, no caffeine, and some fiber. I also stay away from bars with maltitol; this artificial sweetener doesn't sit well in my stomach. It's a fairly common reaction.

No one food is the magic cure-all, no matter what the advertisements say. A balanced diet is better for you than one that takes you from candy-induced sugar high, to post-candy crash, to candy high again.

Carina: Looking After Her Health

Carina is a pastry chef in her home town of Lisbon, Portugal. Her motto is "how can I serve you something if I haven't tasted it myself?" As a result, her pastries are fantastic, but she's about 30 kg overweight. Carina's doctor had been warning her about the risk of diabetes for years but it didn't seem to matter. Then one day Carina saw herself and her sister reflected in a store window. They had always looked a lot alike, but now Carina could barely see a resemblance. That was enough to get her to act.
Working with her doctor, Carina chose 3 simple steps. She would walk at least 15 minutes twice daily. She would only taste one bite of her pastries, and only test 2 of them a day. Finally, she picked 3 raw vegetables that she really liked and made them her standard snacks. She could have as many of them as she wanted throughout the day. That was it!

After 6 months Carina had lost 10 kg, felt much better, and could start to see a resemblance with her sister again. That gave her the confidence to try a more ambitious plan of exercise. Losing weight brought her blood sugar down, reducing the risk of diabetes. Carina took the Singlish steps of setting a goal, making a decision and sticking with it, and it worked. She has promised herself a spa weekend when she reaches her target weight, as a well-earned reward.

Staying Active and Involved

Feeding your body is important. Moving your body and feeding your mind are also necessary if you want a full, active, Singlish life. What's the point of putting all that delicious healthy fuel into your body if you don't make use of it? Here are a few ideas about putting some more fun into your life, in ways that will help you live well, and maybe live longer.

Find some kind of exercise or movement that you like, then do it. Moving around feels good, and it is good for you. We evolved to walk around, not to sit on our butts at a desk or in front of a screen. Almost any kind of movement is good; it doesn't have to be intense exercise, and it doesn't have to go on for hours. A 15-minute walk at lunch time can change your whole day.

Listen to your body to find the right movement for you. Some people like high energy activities; these are the people who look forward to a fast run or a spinning class. Others prefer calmer activities, like yoga or Tai Chi. Personally, I like to walk outside. Just figure out whether you like yoga, jogging, swimming or biking, or something else…and do that. The important thing is to get off your buns and move. If something hurts (I mean really hurts, not just the burn of good exercise) stop doing it immediately. Ask a doctor or trainer for advice, and keep listening to your body to find the best way for you to stay strong and flexible.

We women need to look after our bones, too. A bit of strength training now can not only help your muscles stay strong, it also keeps your bones stronger. Our bones reach their maximum density sometime in our 30s. After that, despite the best diet, supplementation, and exercise, they just don't get any stronger. And when we get older, our bone density decreases; by the time menopause comes and our estrogen levels drop, it's hard to build them back up again.

Start doing something for your bones early; you'll thank yourself later. For some strange reason, I like training with free weights, so that's what I do. I read health magazines for ideas and then try them out to keep the workout interesting. Music and podcasts help me pass the time, or I just let my brain wander with the headphones blocking out the world. I try to exercise 3 times a week, but don't beat myself up if it's only once or twice. I get out for a walk almost every day, and if the weather is terrible I can always turn on music and dance around my apartment. Each day is a new opportunity.

Studies in psychology, neurology, cardiology and other areas have shown that exercise has a positive effect on everything from how well your brain works, to how well your heart works. There's even a study showing that people who exercise regularly handle stress at home, at work, and between the two, better. [9,10] Besides, getting your body moving makes you feel good. So have some fun, do yourself some good, and move.

If you're not sure what your body can handle, talk with your doctor before starting.

What hobbies do you do regularly, just for fun? They can be group or solo activities and can be mentally or physically easy or challenging. Mine include needlepoint or crochet, baking, and model trains (my dad and I can spend hours talking about what the layout should look like, and messing around with the trains to get them running). Whatever your hobbies are, the important thing is to have some. They keep your brain engaged, give you social contacts and keep the days interesting when you stop working. Plus, they are fun!

Hobbies and other relaxation activities also give your brain time to rest and recharge. Did you ever notice that when you have a problem, if you start doing something else and stop thinking about it, the answer will sometimes pop into your head? Dr. Barbara Oakley calls this *diffuse thinking*, when your unconscious mind works on a problem and your conscious mind relaxes.[34] It's real, and having a hobby can make it easier for you to access your diffuse thinking skills.

Think about what you enjoy, or what your favorite playtime activity was when you were a child. It's amazing how much fun we deny ourselves because we are now "too old." Who says there's an age limit on enjoying yourself? If you loved the trampoline as a child, get back on it! Join a local singing group, learn to play an instrument, join a walking or reading group. Anything that gives you pleasure is good. An extra benefit is that you can meet new friends through your hobbies, and you already have something in common. If you are an introvert, or even a little shy, this can make it easier to start a conversation. Promise yourself some fun this week; why wait?

Rest And Recharge

A good night's sleep

Sleep gives your body and your brain time to rest and recover. It's the foundation for having enough energy for your busy Singlish days, and an important part of any overall health plan. It's simple: if you want to function at your best, look good, feel good and think clearly, you have to get enough sleep.

Depriving yourself during the week and then spending the weekend in bed is not the way to do it, either. You can't store up sleep; you need to get enough sleep every night. What's enough? Well, start from 8 hours a night, and then see if you need more.

Take this seriously; chronic sleep deprivation has some serious side effects. It can affect your blood pressure, or your risk of certain heart conditions.[9, 15] Even after only short periods of disrupted sleep patterns, sleep deprived people have been shown to look more fatigued, with reddened or swollen eyes, dark circles under the eyes, or wrinkles around them.[42] When you're tired it shows, and that can impact how you feel about yourself, and how other people treat you. Sleep deprivation makes it harder to think, to make difficult decisions, and to control your emotions.

Tired people feel worse, look worse, and think worse than when they have had enough sleep. Singlish women know that they need to show up in the world at their best every day, because their decisions have consequences. They look after their health, and that means getting enough sleep.

Fortunately getting a good night's sleep can be relatively easy. Think about a few things: what relaxes you? Do you prefer to sleep warm or cool?

Do you need complete dark or can you put up with a bit of light? What about sound?

Make your evening routine and bedroom into a haven for sleep. Change the thermostat or add an extra blanket. Get a white noise machine or a sleep mask. Ban phones, laptops and tablets from your bedroom. Constant connectivity and screen light make it harder for your brain to shut down and stop scanning for input.

Instead, create a routine that signals your brain and body that it is time to relax and rest. Common evening routines include a bath or shower, light reading, listening to relaxing music, drinking a cup of tea or warm milk, or a few minutes of deep breathing or meditation.

Find what works for you, then do it every day. Try to go to sleep and wake up at roughly the same time every day. Keep it simple, so you can do it when you travel. Before long you'll find that your sleep is more restful and you have more energy the next day. When I'm getting enough sleep, I wake up at my normal time with no alarm. The day is much nicer when it doesn't start with a buzz!

Power napping

Have you ever been seized by a powerful urge to just to nap for a few minutes? Ever experience "head bobs" in meetings or in class? An increasing body of research shows that napping can actually be helpful, particularly for people who need to stay very alert, like pilots, or are unavoidably sleep deprived, like people who travel across time zones regularly. [19, 31]

That's what happened to me. I was changing continents almost weekly for my job. By about 2 PM local time, I was barely able to keep my eyes open, let alone contribute to a discussion. Not the image I wanted to project at work! So, following a Tignum tip, I started to nap. I would lie down for about 20 minutes on the floor of my office and sleep. I awoke refreshed, able to function, and feeling far better than if I had eaten a candy bar and pushed through.

Napping is better for you than a cup of coffee. In a study comparing the impact of caffeine, napping, and a placebo on the performance of certain tasks, motor learning was worse with caffeine than with naps and placebo. And participants performed better on memory tests after napping, than after caffeine or placebo. While caffeine can make you more awake, it can't beat naps or a good night's sleep for helping you to be productive.[32]

For a Singlish woman who values her career, a power nap can be a powerful tool. Try one and see how you feel.

Stress relief

Everyone has stress in their life; the Singlish woman is no exception. Where she differs from lots of other people is that she takes steps to manage and reduce it.

First of all, the Singlish woman understands stress. Did you know that there are 2 kinds of stress, *Eustress* and *Distress?* Anything can be a stressor: moving, changing jobs, a fight with a friend, you name it. Most stressors are beyond your control; they are part of participating in the world. The secret is in how you react.

Eustress, or "good stress," is a term first used by an endocrinologist, Hans Selye. It's the positive response you have to something that stresses you: the feeling of excitement when you take on a new job, or the satisfaction when you realize that you understand your finances, even if they aren't in the best shape. Eustress is really more about how you respond to a stressor than what the stressor is. The goal has to be a little bit hard to reach, but not impossible: you can see it but have to stretch to get there. And it takes place over a relatively short period, so you feel the accomplishment before too long.

Think back to a time you had something hard or stressful to deal with: maybe it was a tough assignment at work or at school, or a difficult conversation you had to have with some-one. Once you set your mind to do it, it probably went better than you expected, right? And you felt pretty good about yourself and your abilities when it was over, too. That's a eustress response! It's very Singlish, and it's worth celebrating. Remember that the next time the world throws you something you don't expect. You can do it!

Distress, on the other hand, is what happens when a stressor lasts, and you can't or don't adapt to it. You keep trying to fit 20 hours of activity into 16 hours of being awake, and blaming yourself when you can't finish it all. It is physically and mentally hard on your body and mind. Distress can make you anxious, depressed, tired, or short-tempered. You probably know what this feels like too.

When stressors happen, the Singlish woman relies on her internal strength. She uses the Singlish principles of sticking with her decisions, knowing what she wants, and willingness to try, to shift into eustress. When she succeeds, she celebrates. She also recognizes that some things are just impossible, tells herself the truth about that, and doesn't beat herself up for not being perfect.

Now, I know that we can't handle every stress that easily. Singlish women are still human, and we have bad days, stressful days, down times. Work and relationships have certainly given me some distress over the years. The key is to find out what helps you relax and recover. Your hobbies and movement program play a part here, but so does the special treat. I love massages and try to get one at least every couple of months. I have also tried yoga and meditation. Neither of them works particularly well for me, but they do for many people. Nowadays, yoga and meditation apps and courses are available for free online. Anyone with a connection can access them.

Pets

Do you have a pet? Are you a dog person? A cat person? A bird person? A lizard or turtle person? Pets are great company. They always want to spend time with you. You can tell them anything. Pets don't care if your hair is a mess, or what your bank balance is, or whether you messed up your presentation at work. They are happy to listen, and they won't give away your secrets. They can also make you laugh, and they can even be good for your health! Studies have shown that petting pets can reduce stress, lower blood pressure, and even reduce the number of doctor visits a person makes.[39]

I personally think it's due to a combination of the companionship and unconditional love you get from a pet, the need to take dogs, in particular, for a walk, and the social interactions that just happen naturally between people when there is a pet with them. I see it all the time where I live. Outsiders think the Swiss can be cold or standoffish. I disagree. When someone gets on the tram with a dog, particularly one who clearly adores her owner, everyone on the tram looks at the pet and smiles, then looks at either the owner or another person and smiles again. Pets just make us feel good. Why wouldn't that translate to a happier life?

Please, though, remember that when you own a pet, you are responsible for a life, and it affects your finances and your flexibility. If you can't or don't want to make those trade-offs, try volunteering at a local animal shelter; the rescued dogs and cats there need love too. I can't give a pet a good home now, but when I stop traveling so much I will have either a dog or a Shetland pony. Or both.

Celebrate Your Successes

This Singlish Principle is the easiest one to forget. We get caught up in being busy, or in the day-to-day stresses, and we forget to notice that something really good has happened. Maybe a conversation or meeting went well, or you did better than you expected on a test or in a presentation. Maybe the new recipe you tried was delicious, or your plants flowered in the spring, or you made it to yoga class this week despite being extra busy at work. Give yourself kudos for that. These are all successes, and they deserve to be celebrated.

The Singlish woman knows that she has little victories almost every day, and that lots of little ones add up to big success. So she congratulates herself for them and celebrates her own abilities.

Choose your ways to celebrate. Scale your rewards to the size of the success, so the rewards have meaning. Whether it's a hot bath or a long vacation, reward yourself for something well done. You deserve it.

You can do everything in this chapter. I did, and I'm not the queen of willpower. I just said to myself, "now I am going to do X" and worked at it, until it became part of who I am, not something I wanted to do.

The Singlish woman knows that the way she reacts to what happens in her life is as important as the actual events. This attitude gives her control of so many things that people think are uncontrollable. Think about eating: if you want to start eating better, redefine yourself as the kind of person who doesn't eat fast food. Suddenly walking past McDonalds is no problem. You don't want the fries anyway. Want to improve your public speaking? Start by telling yourself that you can, not that you are afraid to try. If you want to change your habits, use that Singlish self-control to help you stick with your decision.

Lizzie: This one seems pretty easy, I already like to cook; I'm going to try out those recipes you mentioned before. And I like being active; I already do yoga every week, and I like to take long walks. So that part of looking after myself is just a little step from what I do now. I could have more regular sleep habits; too many late night conversations with my roommates right now. And I probably love chocolate a little too much...the truth is, I live pretty well right now. Except for thinking about what it will be like to work, I don't have a lot of stress. And our conversation is helping me deal with that.

Elizabeth: This is a really good start. Focusing on the good parts of your life helps you put the stressful parts in context. Making wise choices, like the ones you are thinking about now, will help you live well later.

Applying Singlish Principles To Living Well

- Plan for now and for later: look after your health now so you can live well longer.
- Tell yourself the truth. If you need to make a change, acknowledge it.
- Stand by your decisions. You know what it takes to live well. Resist pressure to do something that will get in the way of that fabulous life you want to have.
- Celebrate your successes and have fun with your life.

Life Planning for the Singlish Woman

"You can't turn the clock back. But you can wind it up again."

Bonnie Prudden, Rock Climber and Mountaineer

Elizabeth: Now that we have talked about living well in the present, we need to talk about preparing for later in life.

Lizzie: Yes, I guess I should think about this. A few of my friends' mothers talk about how they never expected to get divorced. Now they realize the problem with assuming that their husbands would deal with planning for retirement and getting older. Some of them are really worried. What do I need to do?

Elizabeth: It's good that you are ready to think about this. Lots of women your age prefer not to. Then they get caught out later on, like your friends' moms. The Singlish principles apply here too: plan now for the future, tell yourself the truth.

Lizzie: Wait, I want to take more notes....

Singlish women, it's time to talk about this openly: If you are Singlish, you may live alone to the end of your days. You need plans for the future. Not just plans for a grand retirement with fabulous travel, although that's a good plan to have too. You also need plans to deal with illness, aging, and (since we don't live forever) the inevitable end.

There's no point in putting off these plans; you will have to deal with growing old eventually. Far better to start planning now, before it becomes urgent.

Following the advice in the chapter on Living Well gives you a good start. Eating well, being active, getting enough rest and making time for friends and fun all help you stay healthy as you age. Know your own particular health risks based on your family history and your own state of health, and take steps to minimize them. Live smart, and you can increase the chances that you will live in health for many years.

Planning for your later years begins with just a few simple steps. You owe it to yourself to get started. So let's consider some important points about aging well.

What's Aging? What's Old?

Aging is a normal process. Over time, your body's cells function less effectively or die off, and that changes the way your whole body functions. Your muscles might get a bit weaker or less elastic. Your skin is less elastic and you develop wrinkles. Your hearing might degenerate. Aging happens differently to everyone. Think about the older people you know. I'm sure they have varying degrees of health, mobility, social connections, and happiness.

Aging is nothing to be afraid of. No one can eliminate aging from their life unless they die young. Aging is something the Singlish woman thinks about, as she plans for now and plans for later. You can take some steps right now to influence how well you age.

For your first step, picture what you want your later years to look like. What age do you think of as old? Your answer might change as you get closer to that number. The Rolling Stones used to say "don't trust anyone over 40," but they are nearly twice that age as I write and still rocking. What do you want to be able to do when you are 60? 70? 80? Older?

How do you want to live during those years? Is it important to you to live in your own home until the very end, or would you be comfortable with moving into assisted housing? If you get sick, do you want every possible treatment, or do you believe in letting nature take its course? We saw how important friends and family are to a healthy life. Will moving someplace bring you closer to your friends and family? Would you rather live in a city or a small town?

These are serious questions, and the answer will be different for everyone. Start from your Singlish principles. Decide what you do and don't want. Know what the answers are for you.

Here are my answers to some of the questions. I would like to be independent and able to work well into my 70's if I want to. I don't want to have to work that long. While I'm not particularly afraid of physical illness, I'm terrified of losing my memory or thinking skills, and having to give up my independence. I don't want to have to share my home with anyone I don't know, but I might have to for practical reasons.

When (if) I start forgetting enough things to interfere with daily life, I plan to move into assisted living, while it's still my choice. I'd like to outlive my parents but I don't necessarily want to live be 100, if I can't do it in reasonable health.

My life plan includes moderate exercise to keep my body healthy and my bones strong, cooking most of my food from scratch so I take in fewer chemicals and less fat, and reading and talking with friends, to keep my brain working and my social life interesting. I learned to knit a few years ago; learning a new skill made my brain work in new ways, and completing my first project gave me a great feeling of accomplishment. It was just a potholder for my mother, but it was a big deal for me.

I've also promised myself that if I start to need help getting around, or looking after myself, I will not hide from it. I will take the Singlish road, tell myself the truth, and look for a living arrangement that will give me the support I need, while I can still make the decision on my own.

I didn't need any special course or coach to help me decide these things. I just thought about them in quiet moments, until I had the answers that I knew were right for me.

You can do the same thing. Think about these questions now. Even if they seem morbid. Even though you think you won't need to worry about the answers for a long time. It's much easier to think clearly about them now, before the issues become immediate and emotional. As a Singlish woman, you need to know what your hopes, wishes and expectations are for old age so you can plan to achieve them.

Beyond the basic questions, different tools that can help you with life planning. Various types of insurance and social programs can supplement the money you have saved through your smart Singlish financial planning. Certain legal documents can help ensure that your wishes for your medical care, your financial needs, and even your funeral and what happens to your belongings after you die are all honored.

Too many women hide from these uncomfortable topics, then find themselves in real trouble when aging and illness come into their lives. You, as a Singlish woman, are too smart for that. You can arrange these matters now, so that they are there when you need them.

Insurance

Health insurance

You need health insurance throughout your life, to take care of medical bills if you are sick or injured. Some countries require that everyone pays for a certain basic level of health insurance; anyone who wants more coverage can pay more to supplement it. That's how it works in Switzerland. Some countries, like the United Kingdom, provide national health insurance, where doctor's visits, medicines, and even surgeries are provided free. Actually they are paid for by taxes, but there is no charge at the actual visit. Some countries, like the US, leave it almost entirely up to the individual, with different companies selling different types of insurance to people or to their employers. You will have to work within the rules that are in place wherever you live.

If you can choose your level of coverage, think about what your health risks are, and what care you are likely to need. Then balance the cost of that care against the cost of your coverage, including any payments you might have to make for special care, and decide what makes the most sense. Don't forget about dental care and eyeglasses. Everyone should have their teeth professionally cleaned once a year, and most of us will need glasses as we get older. The right health insurance will help you get the care you need at a manageable cost.

There are two other types of insurance that you should think about: disability insurance and long-term care insurance.

Disability insurance

This is known by different names in different countries, including Disability insurance or Loss of Salary insurance. Regardless of what it is called, it's very important to have. If you are injured or get sick, your medical insurance should cover your medical costs. But what about your other costs? You would normally pay the rent or the mortgage, food, and transportation from your salary. What if you can't work? Medical insurance is generally not designed for these costs. That's where a good disability policy comes in. It replaces the income you lose by not being able to work.

Many countries will have a social insurance plan that replaces a part of your salary. Larger companies may also have a disability plan that will cover you if you are partially or fully unable to return to work. But these generally provide far less than your salary; quite often they are meant to supplement your other resources, not to be the only safety net. Wherever you live and work, learn about what coverage comes automatically, and what policies you can buy to supplement it. Then factor that into your budget and get whatever you can afford. You may never need it, but if you do need it and don't have it, your life can change dramatically for the worse.

The Singlish woman knows that she is responsible for meeting her financial needs. She takes advantage of tools like disability insurance so that she will have enough money if she can't work anymore. She won't be dependent on someone else for basic living expenses.

Long Term Care insurance

Long Term Care insurance policies pay for the cost of care for chronic medical conditions, from help with basic life tasks like bathing and dressing, to more complicated activities that need the skilled attention of a nurse. In the US, most health insurance and government programs only pay for this for a short time. Long Term Care insurance was developed to meet this need, and to help people stay in their homes while still receiving care. These policies aren't for everyone. Talk with a financial advisor and an insurance expert before deciding if Long Term Care insurance is right for you.

In some countries, home nursing visits are part of the national health care program and don't require extra payments. Find out what your government and current insurance will and will not provide. Then close any gaps you find in your coverage.

Having insurance is about making sure that your medical and related care can be paid for. That's really important. It's also important to know and communicate what level of care you do and do not want. If you woke up one day unable to tell anyone what your wishes were, how would they know? The documents we will look at now will help you communicate your exact wishes, even if you can't speak to the doctors, or your family and friends, directly.

Health Care Decisions

Even with the best planning and taking fabulous care of yourself, illness is bound to hap-pen. A good Singlish woman plans for these events in advance. She knows what she wants to happen to herself, and makes sure that her wishes are known.

Two specific kinds of documents are helpful here: a living will and a health care power of attorney. They may have different names in different countries.

The **living will** (also called an advance medical directive) is a way to give specific instructions for your health care, in case you are unable to do so.

Not every state or country recognizes them, though, so contact an attorney for advice and to help you put it together. Even if they are not considered legally binding documents, at least write down your wishes, get them notarized or otherwise legally attested, and make sure the person with Health Care Power of Attorney knows where and what they are.

Be specific; this is no time to mince words. If you want the plugs kept in as long as possible, write it in. If you don't want to go on life support for any reason, write that down. If you want unlimited amounts of pain control even at the risk of a fatal opiate overdose, write that in too.

The **health care power of attorney** lets you choose your health agent, a person who can make decisions for you about your medical care if you can't. Think carefully about this. Choose some-one you trust to make the decisions as you would make them. Talk with them about what those decisions are, and whether they would be comfortable taking on this responsibility. They will need a copy of your living will, and the strength to see that the health care system follow your wishes. Keep a current list of the names, phone numbers and locations of all of your doctors and your pharmacy, along with any medicines you take (prescription and non-prescription) and make sure this person has a copy or knows where it is.

You're preparing for a time when you won't be able to tell anyone what you want; make your documents speak for you.

General Power of Attorney

If you become ill or are injured and can't speak for yourself, who will look after your financial needs? Just like a Health Agent can make your health care decisions, you can designate the person who will make your financial decisions in a legal document. This document is called a Power of Attorney. This should also be written by an attorney, as legal requirements in different states or countries can vary.

The most important part is deciding who will be your agent, or "Attorney in Fact." Who will make the decisions about financial, legal, and life matters for you? Find someone you trust, and who understands what you would want to do in different situations. They might have to sell property, pay bills, represent you in court...it can get pretty complicated. That's why professional legal advice is important.

As you think about the decisions you would want made on your behalf, be specific. If you want them to sell your grandmother's jewellery to raise money for your medical care, say so. If you want the jewellery to go to your niece if you become incapacitated, say that. And say it in writing, because you might not be able to say it later.

Sonja and Gisela

Sonja, 35, is a true Singlish woman, with a career she enjoys, close friends, hobbies, and a Jack Russell Terrier named Ravioli. Sonja and her mother, Gisela, have always been close. In the past 6 months, Gisela began having memory lapses. Her doctor diagnosed early-stage Alzheimer's disease. She started medication, but it will only delay the disease, not cure it. Gisela never planned for this; when she and Sonja's father divorced, there were too many other things to think about.

After a lot of research, Sonja found an appropriate care facility about 20 minutes from her own home. While Gisela was still able to participate in the decision, they sold her house, had an attorney draw up a general power of attorney, a living will, and a health care power of attorney with Sonja as the executor for all of them. They updated Gisela's will, told her friends, and moved her into the new home.

Sonja knew she couldn't ignore her own future needs. She updated her own documents, got Long Term Care insurance, and now has a plan that can be put in place if she becomes ill the way her mother did. It was hard for Sonja to face her mother's illness, and even harder to face her own mortality, but now she feels more in control of her future. Sonja used her Singlish self to face the difficult questions and deal with them. Now she is making the most of the time she has left with her mother.

Your Will and the Snoopy Towel

Everyone needs a will, which lists what you want to happen to your belongings after you die. Many people assume a will is for big things, like money, a house, or jewellery, but it can also be for items of no financial value but great sentimental value. When my grandmother died, I wanted 3 things: my grandmother's opera glasses (bought in a flea market in Paris in the 1950s), my grandfather's pipe (not smoked since long before I was born) and the Snoopy® towel I used when I went to visit them every summer. My request for the towel was actually controversial. Families are funny that way.

If you don't want your descendants fighting over who gets your Snoopy towel, write it down. Choose an executor, who will be responsible for making sure your will is followed. Choose your executor as carefully as you would your Attorney in Fact or Health Agent, and make sure they are willing to do it.

Use a lawyer to make sure your will is legally enforceable (there are kits available but I really prefer a lawyer). If you go to that lawyer with a written list of what you want to give to whom, you will reduce his or her time and thus your bill. Keep your will current and make sure your executor and at least one other close friend or family member knows where it is. Review it every 2 years, plus whenever something important changes in your life: buying or selling a home, having a serious falling out with a planned beneficiary, or maybe even winning the lottery.

Here's another important tip: Whether or not to tell someone that they are in your will and what they are getting is your choice, not theirs. So is the decision of what to give to whom. If you choose to tell your cousin Suzanne that she is not going to get your mother's engagement ring, and she makes a fuss, that's her problem. Give it to whomever you wish.

Funeral Plans

Funerals are already stressful times for the people left behind, and any question about what you would have wanted can lead to big fights. Is that what you want to do your family and friends? Hopefully not! It's better to make your wishes known, in your will or otherwise.

Consider pre-arranging and pre-paying your funeral; that way you know it will be exactly what you want. Specify whether you want to be cremated or buried and where, and what kind of service you want, if any. Buy a burial plot. Some people even write their own eulogy and obituary. My will includes the words I want carved on my tombstone, and instructions for my funeral, so they are (at least in theory) legally enforceable.

I think I will write a farewell letter to be read to anyone who attends my funeral. I like to think of it as having the last word. And it certainly prevents any well-meaning but misguided mourners from announcing that my greatest regret was never marrying, or not having children, or anything else that my friends know is not true.

Lizzie: That's a lot that I haven't thought about. I knew about health insurance, but I've never heard of Long Term Care insurance. I didn't know that Social Security isn't enough to live on for most people. And I thought wills were only for parents and rich people! Where do I start? I feel overwhelmed.

Elizabeth: You can do this. We'll take it one step at a time. Start with the principles. Which ones apply here?

Lizzie: Planning now for later, and telling myself the truth.

Elizabeth: Great, that's the first step. Now, of all the things we talked about, which one do you need first?

Lizzie: I think health insurance. I know I am on my parent's policy, but that will end when I graduate. I don't even know what my current policy covers.

Elizabeth: What can you do about that?

Lizzie: I am going to ask my parents to send me a copy of the policy, so I know what's covered and what it costs and can decide what coverage will be important for me. I definitely need vision coverage; I already wear contact lenses.

Elizabeth: Really good, you are starting to look after yourself. After you sort out the health insurance, what will you deal with next?

Lizzie: As much as I don't like to think about getting badly hurt, I feel very strongly that if am ever in a coma, I want every opportunity to come out of it. So I guess that means the health care directive comes next. And since that needs a lawyer, I might as well do a will at the same time. I don't have a lot, but my friend Sandy really likes my crystal earrings, and I would want my roommate Jennifer to look after my rabbit, Lucy. We've already talked about it, so I know she would do it. She loves Lucy almost as much as I do.

Elizabeth: That is very Singlish of you.

Lizzie: It is?

Elizabeth: Absolutely. You are thinking about hard questions, dealing with them openly, telling yourself the truth and making decisions about what you want and don't want. And you are doing it all much earlier than I did. I was 35 before I made a will; when my friend's dad died, I saw how she and her brothers fought over his book collection. It was enough to get me thinking, and then to call a lawyer.

Life Planning with the Singlish Principles

- Look after yourself. Plan now for the future, including the last part of your life, so you can be healthy and secure until the end.
- Know what you want and don't want. Document your health care and property wishes and update them regularly.

- Tell yourself the truth about getting older; don't hide from hard decisions or uncomfortable topics

It's Not All Wine and Roses

Lizzie: This all sounds so good! You have a career you enjoy, a big group of friends, you even own your own house. You take vacations and do fun things now, and you have a plan for the future. Being Singlish sounds perfect - you make me believe that I can have everything I want in life! Sure it will take some effort, but it won't be that bad. I can do this.
Elizabeth: (laughing) You absolutely can do this! And you are right, I certainly do have a good life! It might seem a little scary now, but overall my life is fun and exciting.

Still, you should know that it's not perfect. There are some days that are not 100% wonderful and we should talk about that too. It's not that I don't have down days, or times when I doubt myself.

Lizzie: No way! I can't believe that you ever had doubts. I have them all the time! I thought that if I lived Singlish that would all go away.

Elizabeth: Well, I wouldn't change much about my life. But I do want you to know what the less than perfect days look like. You will have them, and you will recover from them, and that's an important lesson too. Overcoming tough times builds resilience and inner strength. Some days you might question your choices; this is an important time to be honest with yourself and decide whether it is time to change something in your life. If that's the case, be brave and try.

Lizzie: Uh oh. Can you give me some examples?

Elizabeth: Yes, let me tell you about some of the downsides, and how I deal with them…

Thus far living life as a Singlish single woman has sounded wonderful: all self-determination, confidence and adventure. There is another side to the Singlish life, though, and I'd be remiss if I wasn't honest with you about this part too. Every day is not uniformly wonderful. Like all of us, the Singlish woman has her down days. And there are some aspects of life that just lend themselves better to coupledom. So let's put this out in the open. Here are some of the drawbacks to the Singlish life.

Loneliness

Someday, some time, no matter how busy and fulfilling your Singlish life is, you will wake up, literally or figuratively, to an empty home that seems to echo with the sound of no one else being there. You'll wish for someone to take you to the airport, or greet you when you return, or join you for dinner or a walk in the neighborhood, or for someone to listen and understand when you have a particularly good or bad day. That's normal, and it's even healthy. After all, it means that you are still interested in connecting with the outside world.

I've had my share of lonely moments when I longed for someone to be around, and those moments stink. I've moped around the house over it, even cried myself to sleep sometimes. During those moods I re-examine my decision to stay single – is it time to give up some my independence and turn my attention to finding a man? Should I contact a matchmaking service this time, or try another dating app? Thus far I've always decided that no, I still want my single, Singlish life.

When your down day comes, don't look at it as a sign that your life is terrible, that your choices were bad, that your critics were right, and that you need to devote your life to someone else in order to find happiness. Just go with it for a while. I really believe in the therapeutic value of the occasional good cry.

Then take a deep breath, think about what you want from your life and whether you are getting it, and go on from there. Everyone gets the blues sometimes – Singlish or not. Dealing with them, and coming out the other side, helps you grow stronger and know yourself better.

Awkward Comments

These can be positive or negative. Women, especially, may be conflicted about your choices, perhaps because they might have wished to make different choices themselves. So they might say things like "Your life is so easy, you have no one to worry about" or "Don't you wish there was someone there to do X for you?" People may ask "But when will you have children?" or "How could you disappoint your parents like that?" or "Are you a lesbian?" or even "What made you hate men?"

Yes, these are all real questions that people have asked me, sometimes over and over. In general, I find that awkward questions come from a few areas:

Different generation/culture

These people honestly don't understand. Be gentle with them when you respond.

People who feel threatened

Your Singlish existence (and your satisfaction with it) casts doubt on a central tenet of their own worldview. It frightens them. The question about hating men came from someone like this. So do the occasional comments about how God will punish me. I ignore those; they are not worth the oxygen spent on the response.

People who can't help stirring up trouble

It's not their fault, it's a character flaw. Have a little fun, make up a flippant answer. Just don't be mean.

People who are jealous

Some women, and some men, look at your life and think, 'I wish I had been brave enough to do what she did.' But they can't say that, out loud or to themselves, and they certainly can't imagine that they could still make changes in their lives. Instead, the envy comes out as attacks. They might make snide comments like 'that must be a nice problem to have!' or 'I bet it sucks to be you' when you mention something about your life, whether positive or negative.

Don't take it personally. Their choices were their choices, and if they stay in their unhappy situation, that's a choice too. Your choices were your choices. You live your life, they life theirs.

Doing It All Alone

Let's face it, some things are harder to do alone. Not impossible, just harder. Organizing a move comes to mind, perhaps because I've done it so many times. There are a million details to keep straight: dealing with closing the current home (terminating the lease or selling the property), packing, putting things in storage, finding a new place, then setting up new bank accounts, finding the grocery store, local pub, dry cleaner. They all take a lot of time, and when you are working, that time is hard to come by. At times like these, I've often wished for someone to take care of these details so I could get on with the big stuff, like earning the paycheck that makes it all possible. Somehow, I always muddle through. It might take me a little longer to find the perfect local hangout spot, but I manage it eventually.

Or it could be something smaller, like redecorating, or planning a big event.

I've learned to take help where it is offered, to not worry quite so much about instant perfection, and to "go with the flow" a little. I plan, and I am honest about when it makes more sense to hire help or ask a friend.

The lesson here is to plan what you can and get help when you need it. Find some small way to treat yourself and then get on with things.

Self-Doubt

One day you wake up and wonder of you have made the right decision. Should I really have taken that job? Can I really afford the house I just bought? Maybe I should have kept my old car going with repairs for another year. Everyone has doubts. The Singlish woman doesn't necessarily have a partner to talk through those doubts with her, but she does have friends. She can rely on them to give her honest opinions.

While talking about your doubts with your friends, remember these Singlish principles: Know who you are. Know what you want. Have fun and celebrate your successes. Most importantly, always tell yourself the truth. Most of the time, you will find that your decision was the right one. If so, celebrate the success of reaffirming it. If it really looks like you need to make a change, don't be afraid to try.

Needing Help

Most of us can learn to do basic jobs around the home: painting, changing light bulbs, hanging pictures, digging a garden, cleaning the garage. Even repairs to windowsills and changing light switches are easy to master. There are many resources: classes at local community centers or home and garden shops, TV shows, online courses or videos can all teach you how to do something new. You will be amazed at what you can learn, and it's great for building your confidence, too.

Still, there will be some things you can't do on your own. That doesn't mean you're not capable. Be honest with yourself: if you know nothing about plumbing, don't mess with the leaking faucet. Instead, reach out to a capable friend for help. These can even turn into fun events. I once helped a friend carry a very heavy carpet down her narrow and twisty staircase. We suffered and grunted and nearly dropped it a couple of times – and we still laugh about it today!

Don't hesitate to ask. You're not giving up your independence. And besides, they are your friends, right? Friends are there for one another.

For jobs beyond your friends' capabilities, or something really serious, hire a professional. Get references, check out their reputation with the local business complaint organization or online services like Angie's List (US) or checkatrade.com (UK) or your local equivalent. Then get a few quotes, hire someone capable and get the job done. It is worth the money to have it done right.

Elizabeth: So you see, every day isn't perfect, but there are ways to handle the bad days.
Lizzie: This makes me scared and sad. I thought that if I followed the principles it would all be easy!

Elizabeth: You never know what life will bring. There are always going to be some times that aren't as good as others, and no principles can prevent that. The Singlish principles will help to reduce the number of bad days, and if one does happen, they give you the tools to make it better, which makes you stronger and better able to handle the next bump in the road. Having control of your own life makes all the difference.

Singlish Principles for Days When the Roses Have Wilted

- Know who you are. No matter how bad life may look today, you can look in the mirror and see a woman you know, respect and love. That is incredibly powerful.
- Know what you want. On a down day, you can look honestly at your choices again and decide whether they are still the right ones for you.
- Tell yourself the truth. If something isn't going as expected, face that and adjust. Can you rescue it? Or is it really time for a change? You can always find some small way to make it better.
- Don't be afraid to try. If you need to change something in your life, do it. Trying and failing is not the end of the universe, and it is far better than not trying to improve your situation at all. Every step counts.

Common Questions About Being Singlish

"All change starts with a change in the head"

Karen Hagemann, James G. Kenan Distinguished Professor; Adjunct Professor of the Curriculum in Peace, War and Defense, University of North Carolina, Chapel Hill

"Remember always that you have not only the right to be an individual, you have an obligation to be one"

Eleanor Roosevelt

Lizzie: I feel so much more prepared to leave university. I can't thank you enough. But now I have to get ready for my next class.

Elizabeth: I am so happy this helped you. We can talk more any time; I am always here to help you. Is there anything else you want to ask today?

Lizzie: I would like to ask you a question: what other tips do you think I should have right away?

Elizabeth: Yes, there are a few more things I wish I had known at your age. Think about these until the next time we talk…

When I talk with people about living Singlish, I often hear these questions. Here are the answers. If you have other questions, you can email me (mplatt@fundamentalcapabilities.com) or contact me on the Singlish Facebook page.

I want to live Singlish, but I'm not wealthy and don't have a lot of education. What can I do?

Singlish life doesn't require a lot of money or education. It's really about how you approach the world, and what decisions you make. If you take control of your life, make your own decisions rather than do what anyone else thinks is right for you, stand up for your-self, and make your own plans for your life, you are living Singlish.

Here are a few tips for living a Singlish life that don't cost much:

Reading and education

I am a big believer in self-education and learning by a combination of reading and doing. New books can be expensive, but many towns have used bookstores, and most also have free libraries. Make these your primary source for books, and supplement with new books purchased on sale in stores or online. You may have to wait a little bit for a book to be available, but you will save a lot.

Similarly, community colleges, local universities, and even public libraries host lectures or short courses in various topics. I've attended lectures on history, marketing, and politics, among other things. After the lecture, go and talk with the speaker, and learn even more.

Listen to podcasts or watch YouTube videos from experts. These can help you understand everything from the basics of digital marketing to the latest trends in communication.

Try online learning platforms, like EdX (www.edx.org), Coursera (www.coursera.org) or any of the similar providers. You can find everything from introductory to advanced courses from reputable universities. Most courses offer a statement of completion. Some offer tracks of classes leading to a certification. While not the same as a degree, it still shows that you have demonstrated a level of knowledge about the topic and can help you get a better job. Many of the courses are free, though there may be a small fee for the certification tracks. Beyond that, all you need is computer access, time, and the willpower to complete the course.

As a Singlish woman you have the self-discipline and to achieve your goals. You can do this.

Style and clothing

It's better to have fewer, higher quality items than many items that fall apart after a few months. Fast fashion that you wear a few times and then discard is just a waste of time, money, and natural resources. Shop the sales and outlets and visit better consignment shops in your town. Most importantly, look after what you have. Despite what the label says, most items do not need to be dry cleaned. Keep your clothes clean, sew on loose buttons before they get lost, and press them if they need it.

Perhaps most important, wear bras that fit! Good "foundations" and good posture make every outfit look better. Conversely, if you slouch and sag, even an expensive suit can look sloppy and cheap.

Take advantage of free shopper and makeup consultations in stores, look online and in magazines for ideas, or ask a friend whose style and presence you admire for tips. Watch people around you. If you admire part of another woman's look, ask her about it. Most women will be flattered, and you can get some great tips.

Socializing and entertaining

Singlish women have a variety of options here. If dinner at a restaurant is beyond your means, have lunch, coffee, or a drink instead. Learn to cook or improve your cooking skills; for the price of a single meal in a restaurant, you can often feed four at home.

I personally love my slow cooker. Not only is it easy, but almost any piece of meat slowly cooked will be tender and tasty. There are plenty of free recipes and tips online. I've included a few of my own favorite recipes in the back of this book, too.

Another option for getting together with friends is the "potluck" meal, with everyone contributing one item. If you have a group of friends to do this with, you can have a regular round of get-togethers without any one of them being too expensive.

Not into cooking or group meals? Choose free or inexpensive activities to do together. Go on a hike, or a walk in the park. Participate in community clean-up day together, or even clean the garage. Almost anything can be fun if you have the right attitude.

I want to be Singlish but it sounds like a lot of work to get there. How do I start?

Living Singlish first requires an attitude change. If you really want to do it, you can and you will.

Start by looking at your habits and how you make decisions. Pick just one to work on. Make it something easy so that you can see a success. Maybe it's deciding on a financial goal and starting to put aside some money towards it every month. Maybe it's deciding to take one online course about something you are really interested in doing, or to improve your skills for work. Maybe it's telling your neighbor that you really don't want to visit with her every day because you have errands to get done. Whatever it is, decide what you want to do, and celebrate every step along the way.

If you have a lapse, don't be angry at yourself. Remember, getting to Singlish is a journey and you don't get there all at once.

Try going Singlish with a friend, so that you can encourage one another. Or find a woman who you think is already living this way and ask her for tips. She may not call it Singlish, but if she makes her own decisions, plans for her own life, and generally seems to follow the Singlish principles, she can be a great mentor or role model.

Most important, be true to yourself. There's a strong, capable woman in each of us; all we need to do is let her out.

Email me (mplatt@fundamentalcapabilities.com) and tell me your story. Join our community on Facebook or Twitter. There are thousands of Singlish women out there ready to share their stories and support you.

I'm married, can I still be Singlish?

Yes! Singlishness is about attitude, and confidence, and making your own choices. It's independent of relationship status. Your spouse is your partner. You are both equal. You can have a fabulous Singlish life by following the 7 principles whether you are married or not.

I'm a mother, can I still be Singlish?

Absolutely. I think it's important for children to see Singlish moms as role models.

Women now have more choices about how to become a mother and raise their child(ren). You might raise that child alone, or with a husband, an unmarried male partner, a woman to whom you are married or partnered, or in another kind of relationship. What's important is that it works for you, and gives your child a loving home.

As a Singlish mom, you are a great role model. Every day you will show your child what women can do: be responsible for themselves and others, make good choices, stick with their decisions, plan for now and the future, and be full citizens of the world.

You can raise another Singlish daughter, or a son who understands and values women as fully competent and equal individuals. If enough women raise Singlish children, perhaps we won't need books like this anymore.

That's not to say that it will be easy. You will need all of your Singlish skills and attitude to be successful. Children need a stable, loving home. They also need food, clothing, vaccines, help with homework, support and discipline. They need to be taught how to get along in the world. That's a lot of work, and there is only one chance to do it right.

You will have to balance your own needs, your work and your social life, with the needs of your child. Your Singlish skills will help you adjust your goals and reach them, make decisions and stick to them, and tell yourself and your child the truth.

Is being Singlish just for young women?

Not at all. The Singlish attitude can serve you for your entire life. As you move through different life stages, the challenges can change, but the principles that help you overcome them remain the same. I've been Singlish for many years, and I still refer to the principles every week.

How do I find other Singlish women?

Singlish women are all around you: in your family, among your friends, neighbors and colleagues. Even the women you see in local businesses, like the grocery store, or the dry cleaner, or the coffee shop, could be Singlish. Get to know them and find out.

You can also find Singlish women by joining our Facebook or Twitter community.

Lizzie: I can't believe how long we've been sitting here. I need to go to class! Can we meet again? I want to talk about these questions, and I am sure I will have more.
Elizabeth: Sure, we can meet again any time. I'm inside you; just look for me.
Lizzie: Thank you so much! How about next Saturday morning? I can meet you here for coffee...

Start Your Singlish Life Now

"I didn't get here by dreaming about it or thinking about it – I got here by doing it."

Estée Lauder, Founder, Estée Lauder Companies

Congratulations – you have finished your introduction to the Singlish life! You have seen how a few simple principles can help you shape your future. You have what it takes to be Singlish.

So…now what? Well, if all makes sense to you, jump in and get started. Set your goals, make your plans, and build the life you want.

There's a community of Singlish women out there, who are just like you. Check in with us on

Facebook or Twitter and tell us how you are doing. Share your stories. We're here to cheer you on!

Or maybe it's all still a bit intimidating for you. Maybe you know that simple isn't always easy, or maybe you are a little afraid, maybe you don't know quite how to start building a Singlish life.

Don't worry, you are not alone. Here's what I suggest:

Put the book down.

That's right, put it down for a day or two, and don't look at it. Instead, think about it. What sections really caught your attention? Which of the women we met did you identify with? Whose story made you think "that sounds like me"? Once you have identified that, you know where to start. Read that section again. Why did it mean so much to you? What are you trying to do that relates to it? Review that chapter's principles and think about them some more.

Do you know what you want and what you don't want as it relates to this topic? Write that down. Write down "I want to develop a personal style that shows people that I am confident, creative and fun." Or write down "I want to own my own home in five years." Or "I want to learn how to ice skate." Whatever your goal is, writing it down helps to make it real.

Next, think about two things you can do to get closer to that goal and write those down. It could be "get rid of all of the black suits in my closet." Or "Put $100/month into my house fund." Or "find a nearby skating rink and look up their lessons schedules." Again, writing it down will make it real.

Then ask your friends to help you. Pick two close friends and talk with them about your goal. Set a deadline for yourself to take your first steps. Then take those steps, and when you have, celebrate your success. When you buy that bright red jacket, show it off to that friend. When you open a bank account to save for your house, celebrate by going to look at some open houses and let yourself dream about what it will be like on the day you move into your own home.

Check in with your Singlish Facebook or Twitter friends, or on my website. Your progress will inspire other women, and their progress can inspire you. One day at a time, one step at a time, one decision at a time, go after your goals. Build the life you want. You can do it. You're Singlish!

If you enjoyed this book, please leave a review at your favorite online retailer. You can also visit www.fundamentalcapabilities.com to join my mailing list, follow Living Singlish on Twitter, like the Living Singlish Facebook page, or follow me on Smashwords or Goodreads.

Appendix 1: Basic Budget Worksheet

This worksheet will show you how your spending compares to your income. Adjust it to fit your needs, adding different income and expenses as needed. Download a free copy on my website, www.fundamentalcapabilities.com/shop

Income		Expenses	
		Housing	
Salary		Rent or Mortgage	
Investments		Heat/Power/Hot Water	
Pension		TV/Intenet/Phone	
Alimony		Parking	
Other		Gardener/Landscaping	
Total		Homeowner's Association	
		Credit Card payments	
		Student Loans	
		Car Payment	
		Other Debt	
		Gas or Commuting	
		Food and Groceries	
		Entertainment	
		Clothes	
		Pet food	
		Fitness	
		401K or IRA	
		other	
		Car Insurance	
		Homeowner or Renter Insurance	
		Health insurance	
		Travel	
		Total Expenses	

Appendix 2: Choosing Your First Home

This list covers both renting and buying a house or apartment (flat or condo). As with the budget template, modify it to fit your needs. Download a free copy on my website at www.fundamentalcapabilities.com/shop

Item	Must Have	Nice to Have
Type of Home (apartment, stand-alone home, multiunit home)		
Desired towns or areas		
Garage or off-street parking		
Number of bedrooms		
Number of Bathrooms		
Gas or electric kitchen		
Nearby public transport		
Distance to shops		
Washer/dryer (or hookup) in home		
Elevator/lift access		
Garden or balcony		
Commute time to work		

Appendix: 3 Easy Recipes for the Singlish Cook

Eric Klinenberg, in his book Going Solo, writes that learning to cook is about learning to take care of yourself.[27] I agree. Good food prepared at home is an easy way to give yourself the gift of health, the gift of good taste, and (from time to time) the gift of dessert.

Cooking is also one of those skills that can be as hard or as easy as you want to make it. I prefer easy recipes that look impressive, and I have a list that I go to regularly, whether to treat myself or friends, or to wow friends, family, or colleagues. All of them are simple, requiring basic cooking items (usually one pan or baking dish, a knife, and a spoon for stirring and serving, but no more). None require fancy techniques or fancy equipment. Nor do they require special or expensive ingredients.

These are some of my favorite and most reliable recipes. Some of them are derived from those in cookbooks, and I have given credit to the original author, though my versions tend to evolve. They are all gluten free, since I happen to be celiac. Try them, change them to fit your tastes, and enjoy!

Grilled Vegetable Platter

This is a great appetizer or platter to serve at a cocktail party or barbeque, and is always popular.

Thinly slice a variety of vegetables. I like to use aubergines (eggplant), zucchini, mushrooms, and perhaps fennel or summer squash. Lightly toss with olive oil , then cook on a grill or grill pan until lightly charred, turning once to get those beautiful grill lines on both sides.

Cut up sweet peppers into big squares; I like to use a mix of colors. Coat lightly with olive oil, then roast in the oven at about 400°F (200°C) until just starting to char.

Assemble the vegetable on a platter. You can also add sun dried tomatoes, or cherry tomatoes that have been lightly roasted with the peppers. Sometimes I add small pieces of mozzarella or crumble some bacon over the top.

Season lightly with salt and pepper, and serve with balsamic vinegar or a light Italian dressing.

Asian-style Slaw

This is a cold salad based on a combination of the Sweet and Sour Slaw recipe and the Hot Diggity Slaw recipe in Jane Brody's *Good Food Gourmet*. I like it for summer potlucks and informal meals because it provides lots of veggies and can substitute for coleslaw or other cabbage salads, without needing refrigeration.

Thinly slice 1 white cabbage and 1 red cabbage. Shred or julienne several carrots and some sweet red or yellow peppers. Put all the vegetables in a big bowl or bag, so that you have room to toss it all in the dressing.

For the dressing, combine about 2 parts cider vinegar to 1 part soy sauce. Add about 1 part peanut butter (smooth or crunchy, your choice) and 2 parts lime juice. Mix it all up and then adjust to taste. Sometimes I add hot chili sauce, or cilantro. Sweeten it with honey if you prefer. Make sure you have enough to dress the vegetables. Toss it all together, let it sit for 20 minutes or so and then enjoy. This salad will last for several days (if you don't eat it) so it's easy to make ahead.

You can turn this into a meal by adding some stir-fried meat, chicken or shrimp. You can also wrap it in rice paper and make spring rolls (I usually add fresh cilantro and green onions when I do this, and sometimes add some finely chopped water chestnuts or bean threads). It's a very flexible recipe.

Salmon Filets in Pesto Sauce

This is a fast and easy favorite. Take a salmon filet and put it in a roasting pan or on a piece of aluminum foil big enough to wrap the filet completely.

Add a few sliced cherry tomatoes, some finely sliced sweet red pepper, and a bit of commercial or homemade pesto sauce. Add a squirt of lemon or lime juice, then seal up tightly with more foil.

Bake at 425°F (220°C) for about 20 minutes. You'll hear the sauce bubbling when it's done. I serve this with rice or potatoes - anything to soak up the sauce!

You can do the same thing but substitute Thai chili sauce or pad Thai sauce for the pesto. It's just as easy, but has a totally different flavor.

Baked Company (or not) Chicken with Lemon and Capers

This is based on Jamie Oliver's recipe for Tray Baked Chicken from his *Meals in Minutes* cookbook.

Start with chicken thighs. They are inexpensive, flavorful and moist, and stand up well to baking. Take the skin off if you want to, it's good either way. Coat the thighs (both sides) with paprika and marjoram or oregano. Place in a baking pan along with a cut-up lemon (I use one lemon for every 4-6 thighs, cut roughly into eighths). Toss in some cherry tomatoes, rosemary (sprigs or leaves) and couple of tablespoons of capers. Add some wine or broth to the bottom of the pan to keep it all moist. Sometimes I put a piece of bacon on top of each thigh, too.

Bake covered at 425°F (220°C) for about 35 minutes, then take off the cover and cook another 10 minutes or so until the bacon is crispy or the thighs are browned.

I serve this with rice, potatoes, or quinoa. It's easy, and it always gets compliments!

Smashed Potatoes

This one comes from my friend Marie, who taught me the basic recipe. Then I played with it a little. It takes some work, but not too much, and it's a real treat. I make this at holiday meals or on cold grey days; it's great comfort food.

Cut small potatoes into chunks of about 2 inches/5 cm. If I'm in Switzerland, I use the fingerling potatoes sold for raclette. In the US I buy small red potatoes. Doesn't really matter, just use small potatoes and leave the skin on.

Toss the potatoes in a roasting or baking pan with olive oil, whole garlic cloves, and rosemary, until everything is lightly coated with oil.

Cover tightly with aluminum foil and bake in the oven for 45 minutes at 425°F (220°C). Then take out the potatoes, gently mush them with a spoon, just enough to pop the skin. Toss with more olive oil and little salt and pepper.

Roast for about 45 minutes more, removing the cover for the last 15 minutes or so, until the potatoes start to get crispy. Yum!!!

Tastes Like Rotisserie Chicken in the Slow Cooker

This favorite is based on a recipe from Stephanie O'Dea's site, www.stephanieodea.com. I found her online when she decided to make her family's meals in the slow cooker every day for a year. Her site is a great resource for recipes, and also ways to live more simply. It's worth checking out.

I think thighs work best for this but it works with any piece, especially those with bones. Coat the chicken pieces with a mix of ground garlic, paprika, chili powder, oregano, white pepper, and whatever else you like. I experiment with this a lot, and use spice mixes or whatever I have just a little bit of and need to finish off.

Put the coated pieces in the slow cooker and turn it on high for 6-8 hrs. The meat will be juicy and tender. Enjoy.

Yes, that's it. You can also remove the skin to make it less fatty, or if you prefer a slightly crispy skin you can put the pieces under the broiler for 10 minutes or so before serving. I normally can't wait that long because it smells so good.

Slow Cooker Pork Roast

I made this one up myself, using bits of several recipes. Start with at least 2 pounds (1 kg) of pork – shoulder, chops, any thick piece of meat (except a ham) will do. Put it into the slow cooker with:

1 sweet potato and 2 carrots cut into small chunks

1 onion cut into small chunks, or some pearl onions (shallots work too)

Fruit in chunks – I have used apples, apricots (fresh, dried or canned), cherries, and blackberries. You need 1-2 pieces of fresh fruit, or one tin of canned, or a couple of handfuls of small fruits. You can use a handful of raisins, too.

1-2 Tablespoons of honey

½ to 1 cup of broth and/or apple cider or apple juice. White or red wine can also be used.

Add Ginger, nutmeg, allspice and cloves to taste. Mace and sage also work well, as does Chinese 5-spice mix.

Cover and cook in your slow cooker for 6- 8 hours, till the pork is very tender. This is good on its own, with rice or broad noodles or even mashed potatoes. It's a very flexible recipe, and a great autumn comfort food.

References and Readings

There are many, many books and articles about living alone, travel, work, cooking, the history of singlehood, and the many other topics we've covered in Living Singlish. Here are the ones that I referred to when writing this book.

Read some, all, or none, as you choose. If you have a favorite, whether or not it's on this list, share it with the Singlish Facebook or Twitter community.

1. Babcock, Linda and Laschever, Sara: *Women Don't Ask: The High Cost of Avoiding Negotiation, and Positive Strategies for Change*. Bantam, 2007
2. Bach, David: *Smart Women Finish Rich*. (Updated and Revised second Edition). Broadway Books, 2002

3. Bigelow, Maurice: *Sex-Education: A Series of Lectures Concerning Knowledge of Sex In Its Relation to Human Life.* The Macmillan Company, 1929

4. Bly, Nellie: *Around the World in 72 Days.* Bretano's; New York: Pictorial Weeklies, 1890

5. Bly, Nellie: *Ten Days in a Mad-House.* Ian L. Munro, 1887

6. Callahan, Michael: 'Sorority on E. 63rd Street,' *Vanity Fair* Magazine, April 2010

7. Catalyst, *Women CEOs of the S&P 500* (December 2, 2020).

8. Cherry, KE et al: 'Social Engagement and Health in Younger, Older, and Oldest-Old Adults in the Louisiana Healthy Aging Study (LHAS),'. *J. Appl Gerontol.* 2013 February 1; 32(1): 51-75

9. Christian, MS and Ellis, APJ: 'Examining the Effects of Sleep Deprivation on Workplace Deviance: A Self-Regulatory Perspective,' *Academy of Management Journal,* 2011 Vol 54. No 5, 913-934

10. Clayton, R et al. 'Exercise as a means of reducing perceptions of work-family conflict: a test of the roles of self-efficacy and psychological strain,' *Human Resource Management* first published online 26 June 2014

11. Colcombe, S and Kramer, AF: 'Fitness effects on the cognitive function of older adults: a meta-analytic study,' *Psychological Science,* Vol 14 No. 2, March 2003

12. Cook, Blanche Weisen: *Eleanor Roosevelt Volume 1, 1884-1933.* Viking Penguin Books, USA 1992

13. Cook, Blanche Weisen: Eleanor *Roosevelt Volume 2, The Defining Years 1933-1938*. Viking Penguin Books, USA 1999

14. DePaulo, Bella, PhD: *Singled Out: How Singles are Stereotyped and Ignored and Still Live Happily Ever After*. St Martin's Press, 2007

15. Dettoni, J et al: ' Cardiovascular Effects of partial sleep deprivation in healthy volunteers,' *J Appl Physiol* 113:232-236, 2012

16. Ehrenreich, Barbara: *The Hearts of Men*. Anchor Books, 1983

17. Ehrenreich, Barbara and English, Deirdre: *For Her Own Good: Two Centuries of the Experts' Advice to Women*. Anchor; 2nd edition (January 4, 2005)

18. Ely R, Stone P and Ammerman C: '*Rethink What you "Know" about High-Achieving Women*,' www.HBR.org, 1 Dec 2014

19. The Energy Project: http://theenergyproject.com

20. Ford, Judy: *Single, The Art of Being Satisfied, Fulfilled, and Independent*. Adams Media, 2004

21. Foxcroft, Louise: *Calories And Corsets, A History Of Dieting Over 2000 Years*. Profile Books Ltd, 2012

22. Frasier, Marian Bostford: *Solitaire, the Intimate Lives of Single Women*. McFarlane, Walter and Ross, 2002

23. Goodwin, Doris Kearns: *No Ordinary Time: Franklin and Eleanor Roosevelt: The Home Front in World War II*. Simon and Schuster, 1994

24. Gotham History Blotter, www.gothamcenter.org/blotter: *A Hot Supper and a Benevolent Berth: Brooklynite John Arbuckle and*

His Deep Sea Hotel, The Jacob A. Stamler accessed 20 April 2015

25. Gould, Joan: *Spinning Straw Into Gold: What Fairy Tales Reveal About the Transformations in a Woman's Life.* Random House, 2005

26. Hanauer, Cathi (ed): *The Bitch in the House: 26 Women Tell the Truth About Sex, Solitude, Work, Motherhood and Marriage.* Harper Collins, 2003

27. Israel, Betsy: *Bachelor Girl: The Secret History of the Single Woman in the Twentieth Century.* HarperCollins, 2002

28. Klinenberg, Eric: *Going Solo: The Extraordinary Rise and Surprising Appeal of Living Alone.* Penguin Books (January 29, 2013)

29. Kunin, Madeleine M: *The New Feminist Agenda: Defining the Next Revolution for Women, Work, and Family.* Chelsea Green Publishing, 2012

30. McKinsey and Company: *Women Matter: Gender Diversity, a Corporate Performance Driver.* McKinsey and Co, Inc. 2007

31. Mednick, SC et al: 'Comparing the benefits of caffeine, naps and placebo on verbal, motor, and perceptual memory,' *Behavioural Research* 2008 Vol 193, 1 79-86

32. Miles, Rosalind: *The Women's History of the World.* 1988, Michael Joseph Ltd

33. Morgan, Nick: *'Power Cues: The Subtle Science of Leading Groups, Persuading Others, and Maximizing Your Personal Impact,'* Harvard Business Review Press, 2014

34. Oakley, Barbara and Sejnowski, Terrence: 'Learning How to Learn' MOOC from Coursera (www.coursera.org)

35. Pew Research Center, August 2020: *Nearly Half of US Adults Say Dating Has Gotten Harder in the Last 10 Years.* https://www.pewsocialtrends.org/2020/08/20 /nearly-half-of-u-s-adults-say-dating-has-gotten-harder-for-most-people-in-the-last-10-years/

36. Pichierri, et al. 'A Cognitive-motor intervention using a dance video game to enhance foot placement accuracy and gate under dual task conditions in older adults: a randomized controlled trial,' *BMC Geriatrics* 2012, 12:74:

37. Rippel, Joerg and Peltin, *Scott: Sink, Float, or Swim.* Redline Verlag, 2011

38. Sandberg, Sheryl: *Lean In: Women, Work, and the Will to Lead.* Knopf, 2013

39. Siegel, JM 'Stressful Life Events of Use of Physician Services Among the Elderly: The Moderating Role of Pet Ownership' *Journal of Personality and Social Psychology* 1990 Vol 58 No. 6 1081-1086

40. Stanton, Elizabeth Cady, in "The Matriarchate or Mother-Age," *National Bulletin*, Feb. 1892; and other lectures and articles

41. Steinem, Gloria: *Outrageous Acts and Everyday Rebellions.* Henry Holt and Co. 1987

42. Sundelin, T et al: "Cues of Fatigue: Effects of Sleep Deprivation on Facial Appearance,' *Sleep* Vol 36, No. 9, 2013

43. Trowmart Inn advertising brochure, Cheltenham Press, New York (Author unknown)

44. US Census data: http://www.census.gov/2010census/

45. Wikipedia.org, Nellie Bly entry, accessed 20 March 2015

46. Wikipedia.org, Queen Latifah entry, accessed 20 March 2015

47. Willis, J and Todorov, A: 'First Impressions: Making up your mind after a 100-ms exposure to a face,' *Psychological Science* 2006 Jul; 17(7):592-8.

48. *'Women In America: Indicators of Social and Economic Well-Being'*, prepared for the White House Council on Women and Girls by the US Department of Commerce Economics and Statistics Administration; Executive Office of the President Office of Management and Budget; Bureau of Justice Statistics; Bureau of Labor Statistics; Census Bureau; National Center for Education Statistics; National Center for Health Statistics; National Center for Science and Engineering Statistics. March, 2011

49. Wong, H et al 'Late-Life Engagement in Social and Leisure Activities is Associated with a Decreased Risk of Dementia: a Longitudinal Study from the Kungsholmen Project,' *Am J Epidemiol*, vol. 155, No. 12, 2002

50. Zunzunequi, M et al, 'Social Networks, Social Integration, and Social Engagement Determine Cognitive Decline in Community-Dwelling

Spanish Older Adults,' *J Gerontol* B Psychol Sci
Soc Sci Mar 2003; 58(2): S93-S100)

Acknowledgements

Thank you, each and every one of you, for welcoming 'Living Singlish' into your life. If it helps you create the life you want, when you want it, and how you want it, you will have fulfilled my dream for you. I am grateful for your trust.

This book would never have reached your hands were it not for the support of some very wonderful people. I'd like to thank them here:

Patti Milligan of Tignum and Christine Turner of Edward Jones, who shared their expertise so generously when reviewing the Living Well and Personal Finance sections, respectively. Agnes, Sue, Karina and Diana for reviewing sections and making suggestions. Silvia for not only reviewing sections, but for helping me figure out how to get the message out. My Success Team: Lorraine, Isabelle and Dolors, for holding me accountable for actually publishing. Anelia, for inspiring me to keep writing. Scott, for being a Singlish Woman at heart, and my first editor. Marie, Liz, and Jen - too much to say here. And of course Mom, Dad, my sister, and my grandparents…for support, lessons, and examples throughout my life.

Last of all, I'd like to thank all of the women who shared their stories, ideas and dreams, who told me that I was on the right track, and who helped me to get here. I still can't quite believe that I'm a published author!

Successful Singlish Wishes to You All!

About Marne Platt

Thank you for reading Living Singlish. Before you start building your fabulous life, please visit your favorite online retailer and leave a review. Help me spread the word to other women like you.

Reach me on the Living Singlish Facebook page or at www.fundamentalcapabilities.com

Follow me on Twitter: @LivingSinglish

Favorite my author page on Smashwords

Follow me on Medium

Author Bio

Marne Platt is a veterinarian with an MBA, a sense of adventure and strong belief in self-reliance. She has lived in 4 countries (so far) and loves having friends of all ages all over the world.

Marne learned from a young age to navigate life with confidence and poise. Her parents instilled in her a strong intellectual curiosity, which she continues to cultivate while traveling the world for both business and pleasure. She loves meeting new people, learning about new places, reading, writing, chocolate and of course, animals. Marne is passionate about sharing the lessons she learned about Singlish living, climbing the career ladder and making the most of life.

Other Books by Marne Platt

Professional Presence: How to Look, Sound and Act Like a Leader in Any Job (Co-authored with Cindy Steiner)

PREP for Success: How to Position Yourself and Your Requests to Get the Answers You Need (Co-authored with Cindy Steiner)

Available worldwide from your favorite online retailer or at www.fundamentalcapabilities.com